THE
OVERCOMING
LIFE

JIMMY EVANS

THE OVERCOMING LIFE

AS A BELIEVER, VICTORY BELONGS TO YOU.
BUT YOU STILL HAVE TO CLAIM IT.

Content taken from sermons delivered by Jimmy Evans at Trinity Fellowship Church, Amarillo, Texas (tfc.org/watch-read/messages) and at Gateway Church, Southlake, Texas (gatewaypeople.com/watch/message).

March 28, 2010	Overcoming Rejection
April 4, 2010	Overcoming Fear
April 11, 2010	Overcoming Comparison
April 18, 2010	Overcoming Shame
April 3, 2011	Overcoming Unforgiveness
April 10, 2011	Overcoming Discouragement
April 17, 2011	Overcoming Sickness
April 24, 2011	Overcoming Doubt
April 21, 2018	Overcoming Rejection
April 28, 2018	Overcoming Unforgiveness
May 12, 2018	Overcoming Comparison
May 19, 2018	Overcoming Sickness

ISBN: 978-1-949399-39-4 Hardcover
ISBN: 978-1-945529-78-8 Paperback
ISBN: 978-1-945529-79-5 eBook
ISBN: 978-1-945529-80-1 Spanish paperback
ISBN: 978-1-945529-81-8 Spanish eBook

Translations are forthcoming in Chinese, Hindi, Portuguese, Arabic, French, and Hebrew.

We hope you hear from the Holy Spirit and receive God's richest blessings from this book by Gateway Press. We want to provide the highest quality resources that take the messages, music, and media of Gateway Church to the world. For more information on other resources from Gateway Publishing, go to gatewaypublishing.com.

Gateway Press, an imprint of Gateway Publishing
700 Blessed Way
Southlake, TX 7692
gatewaypublishing.com

Printed in the United States of America
18 19 20 21 22 — 5 4 3 2 1

The message of *The Overcoming Life* is desperately needed by a new generation of believers who lack a solid foundation of faith in the promises of God. This book will be a source of great encouragement for anyone feeling defeated or overwhelmed in life as well as an effective tool for those wanting to share Christ with others.

DR. RICE BROOCKS
Every Nation Ministries
Author of *God's Not Dead*

Victory is the birthright of every believer. What a powerful statement. Jimmy captures what it means to see all of life as a child of the King and as overcomers in ALL things, and especially rejection. There is not a greater discouragement than to be rejected by those whose opinions matter most. Jimmy helps shift the focus off of pleasing man to living for an audience of One. Not only will you find stories and examples in this book that ring true for your own life, you will find solutions and a strong scriptural foundation for victory that we have come to expect in all of Jimmy's teaching.

JENTEZEN FRANKLIN
Senior Pastor, Free Chapel
New York Times Best-Selling Author

Praise for *The Overcoming Life*

Jimmy Evans has a unique ability to communicate God's Word in an authentic, relatable way that will transform your heart. In his powerful new book, he shows us how to see our struggles through the lens of faith, sharing practical and biblical insight that transforms pain into purpose!

MARCUS AND JONI LAMB
Daystar Television Network

The Bible tells us that we are more than conquerors in Christ Jesus. If you're like most people, though, you don't really believe it. Just as elite weight lifters rely on spotters to push past plateaus and marathon runners lean on trainers and nutritionists to break through their endurance walls, followers of Christ need spiritual coaches to break through the strongholds in their lives. Buy this book and let overcomer and author Pastor Jimmy Evans guide you to new power, clarity, joy, and purpose in Christ.

REV. SAMUEL RODRIGUEZ
President of the National Hispanic
Christian Leadership Conference

In *The Overcoming Life*, Jimmy Evans provides a practical guide for experiencing victory in the daily trenches of life's battles. Drawing on God's timeless promises in Scripture as well as his own unforgettable stories, Jimmy shares powerful principles that will encourage your heart and strengthen your faith. If you're feeling overwhelmed, discouraged, or uncertain about life, you won't want to miss this inspiring manual for spiritual success!

CHRIS HODGES
Senior Pastor, Church of the Highlands
Author of *Fresh Air* and *The Daniel Dilemma*

To those in the local church who faithfully serve the Lord and minister love, hope, and freedom to His flock. You are unknown heroes who change lives and destinies every day. Your reward in eternity will be vast, and you will finally get the recognition you deserve.

TABLE OF CONTENTS

ACKNOWLEDGMENTS

ALL GLORY AND PRAISE to Jesus for saving me in 1973 and setting me free to live in victory.

Thank you to my lovely wife, Karen, for prayerfully supporting and encouraging me in so many ways. I love you dearly.

To my son, Brent Evans, thank you for contributing your creative input to this project. I'm proud of you.

Gateway Church is dedicated to seeing believers set free to receive the victory in Christ that belongs to them. I am especially grateful for Pastor Robert Morris and the leadership team who lead the church with that vision. I also give my thanks to Craig Dunnagan, John Andersen, Kathy Krenzien, Jenny Morgan, Peyton Sepeda, Caleb Jobe, and Cady Claterbaugh at Gateway Publishing for reaching people around the world with the message of this book.

INTRODUCTION

For whatever is born of God overcomes the world.
And this is the victory that has overcome the world—our faith.
Who is he who overcomes the world, but he who believes
that Jesus is the Son of God?

1 John 5:4–5

THE APOSTLE JOHN'S inspirational message about every born-again person having the inherent capacity to overcome the world has never been more important than today. The world he referred to when he wrote those verses was the enemy of everything good; it sought to squelch the work of the Church and the destinies of all believers.

But if John's world was bad, ours is immeasurably worse. Jesus prophesied in Matthew 24:12 that many people would lose their passion for God and love for one another as a result of widespread rebellion against God in the last days. That has happened on a global scale!

In 2 Timothy 3, the apostle Paul warns young Timothy that the end times will be especially dangerous because of the moral degeneration of mankind. He says that people in the last days will be "lovers of themselves, lovers of money, boasters, proud, blasphemers, disobedient to parents, unthankful, unholy, unloving, unforgiving, slanderers, without self-control, brutal, despisers of good" and so on (2 Timothy 3:2–3). And of course, this is the world in which we are now living.

It seems as if the devil is on a rampage, and he has plenty of assistance from ungodly people in seeking to oppress the faith and freedom of believers. But that is where the bad news ends. Regardless of what the devil and the corrupt world throw at us, we can overcome it! That is our birthright in Christ Jesus.

When I received Christ 45 years ago, I was 19 years old and in bondage in every area of my life. I didn't know one Scripture or even one Christian. The church I grew up in was extremely boring and irrelevant. I had never heard one sermon that changed my life or challenged me to be a better person.

As a new believer, I was relieved that I was on my way to heaven, but I had no idea how to live a victorious life on the earth. By God's grace, my wife and I met a group of mature believers who took us under their wings and ministered to us. The result was a miraculous change in our lives. One step and one issue at a time, we learned to put our faith in God's love, His Word, and His power. Today, we live freely as overcomers in every area of our lives.

But I will never forget what it was like to be defeated and overcome. And I will never stop trying to help fellow believers experience victory, just as our precious friends did for us when we were young in Christ.

Most of this book comes from my journey of freedom. The chapters contain practical guidance in how to overcome issues that affect all of us. When I say *overcome*, I don't mean learning to cope or manage problems. I mean **100 percent freedom and victory**. That is what Jesus died and rose again to give us, and it is ours if we will just put our faith in Him.

As you read through this book, you will probably be able to relate to many of the issues discussed. But there may be one or two that really hit home. If so, I encourage you to read through those chapters as many times as necessary and pray through them in your daily prayer time. You may have lived defeated in those areas for so long that it's hard for you to even imagine being free. That is how I felt too. Of course, the devil is always there to discourage us, to tell us God doesn't love us, to whisper that we will never change, etc. He tells us those lies to discourage us and keep us in bondage. But we must refuse his lies and put our faith in God's Word and love for us. As we do, we will see the reality of God's power manifest in our lives as we learn to overcome the world through our faith in Christ.

I'm so glad you've chosen to read this book and begin your journey to becoming an overcomer in every area of your life.

1

OVERCOMING REJECTION

REJECTION MAY BE the most difficult thing for people to overcome. Thankfully, we have a Savior who understands exactly how this feels.

Jesus Was Rejected

From birth to death, Jesus was the most rejected human being in the history of the world.

> For He shall grow up before Him as a tender plant,
> And as a root out of dry ground.
> He has no form or comeliness;
> And when we see Him,
> *There is* no beauty that we should desire Him.
> He is despised and rejected by men,
> A Man of sorrows and acquainted with grief.
> And we hid, as it were, *our* faces from Him;
> He was despised, and we did not esteem Him
> (Isaiah 53:2–3).

Rejection began for Jesus in the womb. Although obviously not unwanted by God or his mother, Mary, this Child was not wanted by His earthly father, Joseph.

Mary's miraculous pregnancy was a scandal because she and Joseph were not yet married; they were merely betrothed. When Joseph found out Mary was pregnant, he decided to call off the marriage—"put her away secretly" (Matthew 1:19)—because he wanted no part in such a scandal. It took an angelic visitation confirming the baby's identity as the future Savior of the world for Joseph to accept Jesus.

Jesus was also rejected by the Roman rulers. When the wise men came seeking the "King of the Jews" (Matthew 2:2), King Herod was enraged to learn that a young boy could threaten his power. He murdered every male child two years old or younger who lived in or near Bethlehem. Because an angel warned Joseph in a dream of the pending attack, Jesus and His parents escaped to Egypt where they lived until Herod's death. Then they returned to live in Nazareth.

However, when Jesus began His ministry in Nazareth, the people rejected Him. They even tried to kill Him. On the Sabbath, Jesus read a passage out of Isaiah and identified Himself as the fulfillment of the Messianic prophecy. When the people realized that this Man from their hometown claimed to be the promised Messiah, they chased Jesus to the outskirts of town and attempted to throw Him over a cliff. Jesus escaped, but even then He did not have the support of His own family. Instead of accepting His ministry and recognizing His miracles, Jesus' mother and siblings thought He had gone crazy and came to get Him (Mark 3:31).

The Jews constantly rejected Jesus, so much so that they demanded His death. Even worse was the rejection Jesus felt from His heavenly Father as He hung on the cross: "My God, My God, why have You forsaken Me?" (Mark 15:34).

Why did God reject His own Son? Because Jesus took our place on the cross. Our sins make us deserve God's rejection, but on the cross, Jesus became sin. He took upon Himself every sin we ever committed or ever will commit. Therefore, God the Father turned His back to Jesus on the cross. Two thousand years ago, God rejected His Son once and for all so that He will never reject us again in eternity. When we put our faith in Jesus, we are accepted forever.

How Jesus Overcame Rejection

Jesus overcame rejection on every level, and He has empowered us to do the same.

- **Rejection never affected His decisions.**
  Jesus did many things even though He knew they would get Him rejected or killed. The fear of rejection never stopped Jesus.
- **Rejection never affected His attitude or the way He treated people.**
  Jesus was stripped naked in front of His mother, and He died the most cruel, shameful death of any human being who has ever died. Yet even as He hung on the cross, Jesus forgave the people who put Him there.

GOD REJECTED HIS SON
ONCE AND FOR ALL
SO THAT HE WILL NEVER
REJECT US AGAIN
IN ETERNITY.

- **Rejection never kept Him from accomplishing His destiny**.
Jesus did everything that God the Father called Him to do, knowing that He would suffer rejection as a result.

Love and the Fear of Rejection

The importance of overcoming rejection cannot be overstated. The devil often uses rejection to control us and keep us from accomplishing God's will. We humans were created by a loving God to love Him and other people. We were made by love, to love. When asked what the most important commandment was, Jesus replied,

> "You shall love the Lord your God with all your heart, with all your soul, and with all your mind. This is *the* first and great commandment. And *the* second *is* like it: 'You shall love your neighbor as yourself'" (Matthew 22:37–39).

Jesus said the whole Bible is fulfilled in these two commandments. In other words, if we live to love God and love each other, we have done everything that God asks.

If love is our greatest need, what is our greatest fear? *Rejection*. Most people fear rejection more than anything else. On lists of fears, public speaking often ranks higher than death. Of course, it is not the actual act of speaking that terrifies us; rather, it is the possibility of mass rejection. It is one thing for a single person to reject you in a private conversation. It is another thing entirely for hundreds or thousands of people to reject you at the same time.

Rejection is also our greatest *scar*. Why? It hurts more than anything else. Most people would admit their greatest pain comes from rejection in their past.

As our greatest fear and our greatest scar, rejection is the devil's number one control point in our lives. When you are controlled by the fear of rejection, you begin to carry a *spirit of rejection*. This is common for those of us who have suffered a lot of rejection in our lives. A spirit of rejection is dangerous because it takes advantage of our need for love and allows Satan to control the way we make decisions, the way we treat people, and whether or not we will do God's will for our lives.

Ways We Can Be Rejected

In order to learn how to overcome our scars and fears, we must first recognize the many different ways a person can be rejected.

Some people experience rejection in the womb. For one reason or another, they were unwanted as children. My own parents had two sons, and they wanted another child—a girl. Back in those days, there were no sonograms, but my mother had decided I was supposed to be a girl. She even had my name picked out: Debbie Dale Evans (after the famous country western movie star and singer). So it was a problem when the doctor at St. Joseph's Hospital in Wellington, Texas, announced, "It's a boy!" My mother had wanted a girl so badly that

AS OUR GREATEST FEAR
AND OUR GREATEST
SCAR, REJECTION IS
THE DEVIL'S NUMBER
ONE CONTROL POINT IN
OUR LIVES.

she did not name me for weeks. Finally, the hospital called and said, "We have to fill out this birth certificate. If you do not name this child today, his name is officially Baby Boy Evans." And that is how I got my name.

Of course, I was not really an unwanted child, but there are too many who are. Some children perceive they are not wanted through lack of eye contact, affection, or attention. Other parents plainly say, "We wish you were never born," "We did not intend to have you," or "You were a mistake."

Adopted children almost always have to deal with rejection at some point. No matter how loving or devoted the adoptive parents are, the adopted children wonder what caused their birth parents to give them up. They ask themselves, "What was wrong with me? What did I do? Why did they not want to keep me?"

Other forms of rejection can include

- not being accepted or loved
- being excluded
- being laughed at or made fun of
- being gossiped or lied about
- being compared in an unfavorable way
- divorce/adultery
- abandonment (physical or emotional)
- abuse (verbal, physical, or sexual)
- neglect
- not being accepted for who I am

Have you ever felt rejected because you could not live up to someone else's expectations? These standards can be physical, financial, social, or spiritual. No matter how hard you try, they are simply out of your reach. Or perhaps you have experienced a chronic lack of employment. While everyone else you know has a steady paycheck, you are just trying to avoid being laid off again. Many people experience relational rejection from a friend, boyfriend, girlfriend, spouse, or someone else with whom they desire to have a relationship. The pain can stem from the end of a relationship or from the refusal of one person to even begin the relationship. Premature death and especially suicide can be huge issues of rejection for surviving loved ones.

Most people have experienced various levels of rejection throughout their lives. Worse yet, many of us have taken up a spirit of rejection. A spirit of rejection is not just the feeling that you have been rejected but that you have been *deeply* wounded. This pain defines you; it is something you deal with every single day. A spirit of rejection controls your thinking and decisions and compromises your ability to function.

Unhealthy Reactions to Rejection

Here are four common but unhealthy ways we react to rejection.

Avoiding the Risk of Rejection

Have you ever said to yourself, "I do not want to be rejected like I was before, so I am not going to try. I will not give my heart away. I will not try to befriend people."

When we have experienced pain in the past, we often make this inner vow: *No one will ever hurt me again.* We refuse to engage in relationships or endeavors that pose a high risk of rejection. Allow me to make this statement, though: God will never use you unless you risk being hurt. I am not talking about being stupid or opening your heart to abusive people or situations. We should never be unwise. What I *am* saying is that all relationships pose risks. Jesus had twelve disciples, and it was one of those men who eventually betrayed Him. But when Judas approached, the Master called him "friend" (Matthew 26:50). Jesus did not close His heart to the person He knew would betray Him. We cannot live like Jesus if all we do is seek to eliminate risk from our relationships.

Some people pre-emptively reject others to avoid being rejected themselves. This is a primary reason for divorce in our culture—"I am going to reject you before you reject me." It is the same with friendships. We want others to be our friends, but we fear they will reject us, so we reject them first. We believe that being the "rejecter" will keep us from being hurt.

Another form of avoidance is lack of commitment. Why are more people choosing to live together without being married? Why are people "hanging out" but not committing to close friendships? The answer is in this lie we tell ourselves: "If I never commit, I cannot be hurt because I did not give my heart away."

Finally, we avoid rejection by conforming to our environment instead of being ourselves. We do need

WE CANNOT LIVE LIKE JESUS IF ALL WE DO IS SEEK TO ELIMINATE RISK FROM OUR RELATIONSHIPS.

to be gracious and loving people; we should never be self-righteous. However, we should also not live like chameleons—just blending into the background. This type of person speaks like a liberal around liberal discussions and then like a conservative around conservative discussions. This reaction to rejection is unhealthy. While you should always be kind, you also need to be able to express your own opinions, even in situations in which rejection is possible.

Reacting in Anger and Aggression

Almost every person becomes more angry and aggressive when they feel like they have been rejected. One study of 15 school shooters found that 13 of the shooters felt chronic rejection by society and their peers just prior to becoming a school shooter.

Many young people who exhibit aggressive or antisocial attitudes through clothing, hairstyle, music, language, or behavior do so because they feel alienated or rejected by some element of society. Many violent crimes are committed by men who are single, recently divorced, or have lost a close relationship with a woman. These men feel ostracized, rejected, or displaced in some way.

While those examples are extreme, rejection wounds all of us and can make us bitter if we are not careful. In marriage, for example, feelings of rejection can cause spouses to become hostile and aggressive toward one another.

Feeling Hopelessness and Despair

We naturally want to be with the people we love. When you are loved and *feel* loved, you will fight to live; it is our most basic instinct. However, what happens to your motivation to live when you feel unloved? Research shows that people who feel rejected, especially those who experience chronic rejection, get sick much more than people who feel loved. They also experience increased mental and emotional problems as well as much higher mortality and suicide rates.

Rejection is devastating to the human spirit, and any time we go through hurt or trauma, the devil tries to take advantage of our pain. Satan is the hurt whisperer. He uses rejection to introduce lies that change the way we make decisions and the way we treat people. He wants to keep us from doing what God wants us to do with our lives.

In Genesis 3 Satan speaks to Eve as a crafty serpent, and he is still crafty today. When you experience the pain of rejection, he sneaks up and whispers lies, such as

- "You aren't worth anything."
- "No one will ever love you."
- "You are defective."
- "Something is wrong with you."
- "You will always be rejected."
- "God doesn't love you."

The devil wants you to believe that these words are your voice, or even worse, God's voice. He speaks these

SATAN USES REJECTION
TO INTRODUCE LIES
THAT CHANGE THE WAY
WE MAKE DECISIONS
AND THE WAY WE
TREAT PEOPLE.

lies to break our hearts and gain control over our minds through the spirit of rejection. We become convinced that we are defective, unlovable, and will never be accepted by anyone.

Being Overly Sensitive and Overly Dependent

I was an *extremely* large child. I was taller than my second grade teacher, and I could beat up everybody in school until I was in high school. My nickname was "Lurch." My brothers knocked my front tooth out once, and when I got a cap on it, they called me "Bucky, the silver-toothed beaver." My brothers tormented me all my life, but I was not the type of person who would talk about how hurt I felt. So I put on a tough exterior, and I fought a lot, including many older kids. I was not afraid of anybody. I would come after anyone who made me angry or rejected me.

When Karen and I got married, I had a spirit of rejection all over me. I was too sensitive, and any little thing Karen would say or do could set me off. To make matters worse, Karen had a spirit of rejection too. We were both very sensitive about every area of acceptance. That is why we fought so much at the beginning of our marriage.

People who carry a spirit of rejection are the most offendable people on the earth. They are sensitive to every single thing that is said and done, like Karen and I were. They become self-centered and self-absorbed, They are also overly dependent upon the approval and acceptance of other people. Ironically, though, people who become overly dependent upon others tend to be viewed as unattractive. It is a no-win situation.

When you are a people pleaser, you will do anything to gain other people's affections, even if it means compromising your morals or standards in order to avoid rejection. As a kid, I had bad friends, and I did bad things like getting drunk, being immoral, etc. I remember thinking to myself so many times, "I really don't want to do this, but I'm afraid of what my friends will do if I tell them no." Peer pressure and the fear of rejection caused me to compromise my morals. We can do the same thing as adults. We really don't like the things we are saying or doing, but we are afraid to stand up for what we believe is right.

———

Most people deal with rejection in one or more of the ways previously mentioned. Tragically, these methods keep us from living in freedom and being the people God created us to be.

How to Overcome Rejection

How can you overcome rejection and not be defined by it for the rest of your life?

Base Your Life on God's Love and God's Word

The first way to help overcome rejection is to base your life on God's perfect love and what His Word has to say about you.

The writer of Hebrews says,

> *Let your* conduct *be* without covetousness; *be* content with such things as you have. For He Himself has said, "I will never leave you nor forsake you." So we may boldly say:
> "The Lord *is* my helper;
> I will not fear.
> What can man do to me?" (Hebrews 13:5–6).

Not one person feels rejected by what God has done. It is what people have done. I love people, but even good people have bad days and go through difficult times. When you live your life based on people's love, you will end up disappointed and scarred.

God promises that He will never leave you and never forsake you. Physically, He will never leave. Emotionally, He will never turn His heart away from you. There will never be a moment for the rest of your life that God is not emotionally connected to you and thinking about you. There will never be a moment in eternity that God leaves you physically.

It is a wonderful blessing to know that our God is absolutely committed. On our worst day, He is our best friend. When no one else is there, He is still there. I know a lot of people have told us that they would "never" leave, but then they left. When we lost our looks or our money or could not give them what they wanted, they

WHEN YOU LIVE YOUR LIFE BASED ON PEOPLE'S LOVE, YOU WILL END UP DISAPPOINTED AND SCARRED.

left. They said they were committed, but good times and words don't define commitment—bad times and trouble do. If you are still standing on the other side, you are committed. When God says "never," He means *never*. He is eternally committed.

The Bible says God's love heals a spirit of rejection because "perfect love casts out fear" (1 John 4:18). When we got married, I had only been saved for a week, and Karen had the lowest self-esteem. We were a mess! Karen thought she was ugly and was convinced God could not love her; she did not believe that she could be saved. But my wife is an incredible woman. Over the four decades of our married life, she has woken up *every* morning and read the Bible and prayed, regardless of the circumstances.

In the beginning, Karen did not even really believe the Bible, except for the passages about hell and judgment. She struggled to believe the Scriptures about God's love, but she continued to read the Bible every day anyway.

Psalm 107:20 says, "He sent His word and healed them, / And delivered *them* from their destructions." Hebrews 4:12 says, "The word of God *is* living and powerful, and sharper than any two-edged sword." One side is the sword to slay the enemies of God; the other is a scalpel to heal us. You do not read the Bible; it reads you. As Karen allowed the balm of God's Word and His love into her heart every day, God healed her from the spirit of rejection. This beaten-down woman who thought she was ugly and unlovable over 40 years ago is now a lioness for God.

YOU DO NOT READ THE BIBLE; IT READS YOU.

I watched God heal my wife, and He also healed me. God replaced my spirit of rejection with a spirit of adoption and acceptance. His Word can heal you too. Read the Bible and pray every day. Like Karen, you may struggle with believing what you read at first, but keep doing it. As you meditate on God's Word, ask the Holy Spirit for healing and power. Jesus overcame sin and death because of the Father's love, and that same love will set you free.

Pursue Relationships with Fellow Believers

The second way to overcome rejection is to pursue relationships with fellow believers who are pursuing God in healthy relationships.

Look for people with the right standards of acceptance. I want to make this clear: nobody is perfect, and Christians are not perfect. However, Christians are *different*. If your closest relationships are with worldly people, get ready for disappointment. Worldly people only love you for your looks, money, position, or what you can do for them. When you lose those things, you lose those people too.

Proverbs 17:17 says, "A friend loves at all times, / And a brother is born for adversity." Here is what I have found about most Christian friends: they are *committed*. When you are struggling, they do not run away—they show up. They have a different value system. You can count on Christian friends more than anybody else not to reject you. They may challenge you. They may stand up to you to keep you from hurting yourself or continuing in sin. But they are faithful. And those two characteristics—a common value system and faithfulness—will help you avoid rejection.

As believers, we should love everybody. We should be friendly toward all people, exhibiting the fruit of the Spirit (joy, patience, and kindness) in our daily lives. Our closest friends, however, should be people we choose very carefully.

Don't Take Rejection Personally

The third way to overcome rejection is to expect it and not take it so personally. You *are* going to be rejected sometimes. After all, Jesus Himself was rejected. In Luke 6:26 Jesus says, "Woe to you when all men speak well of you, / For so did their fathers to the false prophets."

If everyone only has good things to say about you, you may be a pretty cowardly person. You may be a social chameleon, telling everybody what they want to hear for whatever reason. Yes, we should be nice and gracious, but we must also understand something about living in this world: if you stand up for God, you will get beaten up at times. Are you being open about your faith? Don't be self-righteous, but do realize that being a Christian in this world is a dangerous thing.

Luke 6:22–23 says,

> "Blessed are you when men hate you,
> And when they exclude you,
> And revile *you,* and cast out your name as evil,
> For the Son of Man's sake.

A COMMON VALUE SYSTEM AND FAITHFULNESS WILL HELP YOU AVOID REJECTION.

> Rejoice in that day and leap for joy!
> For indeed your reward *is* great in heaven."

Have you ever done that? When somebody rejects you or begins to talk negatively about you, do you jump up in the air and leap for joy? No, that is not what most Christians tend to do. We tend to be hurt and resentful. But if you understood the reward for standing up for your faith, you would be willing to be rejected for your Lord. Jesus says your reward in heaven is great, and when we remember that, we can leap for joy even in the face of rejection.

I am against killing babies in their mothers' wombs. I am against the immorality in the world today. I am against the rebellion in schools and the way children are treating their parents. I am against many things that are going on right now, and I believe the Word of God is the infallible Word from heaven by which we should live our lives. Because I believe those things, I know I am going to be rejected. So be it! I have settled it in my heart.

Jesus overcame rejection because He expected it. He told His disciples, "The Son of Man will be delivered up to be crucified" (Matthew 26:2). Jesus knew He was going to live a perfect life and still be rejected by many people.

Unrealistic expectations set us up for the worst pain. Thoughts like "Life will be easy, and everyone will treat me well" are toxic because they are lies. Be as lovable as you can possibly be but also understand that no one is always accepted. You will be rejected by many in this world if you are a Christian. Replace those toxic thoughts with the truth: "Not everyone will like me. Life isn't always going to be easy. No matter what, though, God always loves me, and He is always with me."

Forgive Those Who Reject You

The fourth way to overcome rejection is to forgive those who reject you and give them God's love and acceptance in return.

In Luke 6:27–31 Jesus says,

> "But I say to you who hear: Love your enemies, do good to those who hate you, bless those who curse you, and pray for those who spitefully use you. To him who strikes you on the *one* cheek, offer the other also. And from him who takes away your cloak, do not withhold *your* tunic either. Give to everyone who asks of you. And from him who takes away your goods do not ask *them* back. And just as you want men to do to you, you also do to them likewise."

You know that you are being controlled by a spirit of rejection when you cannot love a person beyond the way they are treating you. "You are nice to me—I am nice to you. You are mean to me—I will be mean to you. I am going to treat you the exact same way that you are treating me."

That kind of response shows you how weak in spirit we are. But when God's love is flowing inside you, you can rise above your circumstances. You can smile when others are frowning at you, you can love when others are hating you, and you can bless others while they are cursing you. You have overcome a spirit of rejection when you can love people in all circumstances.

––––––––––––

Responding to others in the spirit of love and forgiveness makes us like Jesus. Luke 6:31 says, "Just as you want men to do to you, you also do to them likewise." Some of the most unloving people in the world just need someone to show God's love to them. We can only do that if we have overcome the spirit of rejection.

2

OVERCOMING FEAR

LUKE 22:39–47 RELATES the story of Jesus in the Garden of Gethsemane before He suffered and died.

> Coming out, He went to the Mount of Olives, as He was accustomed, and His disciples also followed Him. When He came to the place, He said to them, "Pray that you may not enter into temptation."
>
> And He was withdrawn from them about a stone's throw, and He knelt down and prayed, saying, "Father, if it is Your will, take this cup away from Me; nevertheless not My will, but Yours, be done." Then an angel appeared to Him from heaven, strengthening Him. And being in agony, He prayed more earnestly. Then His sweat became like great drops of blood falling down to the ground.
>
> When He rose up from prayer, and had come to His disciples, He found them sleeping from sorrow. Then He said to them, "Why do you sleep? Rise and pray, lest you enter into temptation."
>
> And while He was still speaking, behold, a multitude; and he who was called Judas, one of the twelve, went before them and drew near to Jesus to kiss Him.

Verse 44 says Jesus was in *agony*. This English word comes from the Greek word *agonia* and means two things. First, it means great fear or maximum emotional stress. Second, it means a contest or wrestling match—a fight for victory.

As I mentioned in Chapter 1, Jesus was the most rejected person who ever lived on the earth. From birth to death, He was rejected on every level. Likewise, here in Gethsemane, Jesus also experienced more fear than any other human being has ever experienced.

Luke, the author of this gospel, was a physician, and he mentions something that no other gospel writer records: *hematohidrosis*. This is a rare condition in which a person is under so much stress that the blood vessels under their skin constrict, rupture, and empty into their sweat glands. Jesus experienced so much fear and emotional distress in the Garden of Gethsemane that His blood vessels ruptured, and He began to sweat huge drops of blood.

Why do we serve Jesus and love Him so much? He endured for us what no other person has ever endured. Jesus literally took hell upon Himself so we could have heaven. He suffered what no other person has ever suffered, and He experienced more fear than any other person has ever experienced. And He overcame it. In this chapter we will learn how we too can overcome fear.

JESUS LITERALLY TOOK HELL UPON HIMSELF SO WE COULD HAVE HEAVEN.

Why Did Jesus Experience Fear?

The Bible never records Jesus experiencing fear outside this episode in the Garden of Gethsemane. He had been on a boat that almost shipwrecked, but He was not afraid then. In Nazareth, the people tried to throw Him over a cliff, but He was not afraid then either. Why was Jesus afraid now? There are several reasons, the first being His identification with fellow humans.

Jesus Was Fully Human

Remember, Jesus is a human being. It is not just that He *was* human—He still is. He is fully God, but He is also fully man. On the earth, even though He was God, Jesus still lived in a physical body.

> We do not have a High Priest who cannot sympathize with our weaknesses, but was in all *points* tempted as *we are, yet* without sin. Let us therefore come boldly to the throne of grace, that we may obtain mercy and find grace to help in time of need. For every high priest taken from among men is appointed for men in things *pertaining* to God, that he may offer both gifts and sacrifices for sins (Hebrews 4:15–5:1).

Remember this Scripture when you pray. In *all* points Jesus was tempted as we are, yet He was without sin. Jesus can have compassion on those who are ignorant and going astray because He Himself was also subject to weakness. Because Jesus experienced fear on the earth, He can be compassionate for us when we pray.

We all experience fear. I experience fear just about every day. Dealing with fear is one of the major themes of my prayer life: "God, I am concerned about this ... I am fearful about this ..." We have an opportunity to go before the throne of grace every day.

And aren't you glad it is a throne of *grace*? We do not have to get our act together to approach God. You can simply go before Jesus and say, "Lord, I am scared." He knows exactly what you are talking about.

Jesus Knew Everything that Would Happen to Him

We often fear the unknown. Whether you are traveling to a new place or simply thinking about tomorrow, you do not know what is going to happen, so you may feel afraid.

However, if there is anything worse than not knowing, it is *knowing*. Jesus foresaw every time people would slap and spit on Him. They would pluck His beard out. They would put a crown of thorns on Him. They would mock Him and whip Him. They would make Him carry His cross. They would nail Him to the cross. Finally, He would suffer physical death.

Jesus knew that He would become sin and sickness; all the sin of the world and all the sickness of the world would come on His body. The Father would turn away from Him, and demons would feast on Him for several hours. I believe that is why the sky grew black on the Friday afternoon when Jesus died. God the Father did not want the world to have to witness what was happening to His Son on the cross as Jesus became sin.

What was Jesus afraid of? Rejection. Suffering. Humiliation. Jesus knew every detail of what was about to happen to Him, and He was afraid.

When we go before Jesus, our High Priest in heaven, and say, "Lord, I am afraid of being rejected by these people," He says, "I know exactly what you are talking about." When we say, "Lord, I am afraid because everybody in my family gets this particular disease. It is genetic, and I am afraid that I am about to get really sick," He says, "I know exactly what you are talking about." Whether we fear pain, poverty, or anything else, Jesus understands. He experienced every fear right there in the Garden of Gethsemane.

Jesus Was Under Attack by Satan

Satan is the ultimate spirit of fear. Matthew 4:1–11 and Luke 4:1–13 both record that Jesus fasted for 40 days in the wilderness, and Satan came to tempt Him. Jesus won that battle.

You can always tell the nature of a person by how they treat vulnerable people. A good person sees someone who is vulnerable and will help, support, and protect them. That is what Jesus did.

An evil person, on the other hand, sees someone who is vulnerable and preys upon that person. Satan is evil. Luke 4:13 says, "When the devil had ended every temptation, he departed from Him [Jesus] until an opportune time." Satan was waiting for Jesus to become weak, and the opportune time came in the Garden of Gethsemane. Jesus knew He was about to be betrayed by one of His

JESUS KNEW EVERY DETAIL OF WHAT WAS ABOUT TO HAPPEN TO HIM, AND HE WAS AFRAID.

disciples and die a gruesome death. As He cried out to God the Father, Satan attacked Him with a spirit of fear.

The apostle Paul writes, "God has not given us a spirit of fear ..." (2 Timothy 1:7a). Fear is not just an emotion. Fear is a demonic spirit used to control people. God will never use fear to accomplish anything in our lives. In the second half of the verse, Paul lists what God *has* given us: power, love, and a sound mind (2 Timothy 1:7b).

Hebrews 2:14–15 describes it this way:

> Inasmuch then as the children [that is, us] have partaken of flesh and blood [being human], He Himself likewise shared in the same, that through death He might destroy him who had the power of death, that is, the devil, and release those who through fear of death were all their lifetime subject to bondage (emphasis mine).

Satan uses the fear of death to control our lives. Most of us have our own particular fears or phobias, but almost every fear can be traced back to the fear of death. For example, are you afraid of being poor? Most likely, you are afraid of the possible consequences of being poor, such as starvation and death. Are you afraid of heights? No, you are actually afraid of falling from heights and dying. Are you afraid of bugs or snakes? You are afraid of dying. Bugs and snakes can bite you and kill you.

Through the fear of death, Satan holds us in bondage throughout our lives. Now let me tell you the good news: Jesus died on the cross, defeated Satan, took back the power over death, and rose again! Just before He raised

Lazarus from the dead, Jesus proclaimed, "I am the resurrection and the life. . . . whoever lives and believes in Me shall never die" (John 11:25–26).

If you are a Christian, you will never die. You will never experience death. I am not saying that your body will not wear out and expire one day. I am saying that the minute your eyes close here, they open in heaven. The minute you stop breathing here, you start breathing there. The minute your senses dull here, they come alive there. You will never die because you are a born-again believer.

People who fear death and do not understand what Jesus has done live under Satan's control. Jesus defeated death on our behalf. You do not have to live in fear. If you live here on earth, you live for God. If you stop living here and move on to heaven, that is even better. It is a win-win deal for every believer.

Jesus experienced fear so He could relate to us. He can intercede on our behalf as our High Priest in heaven because He experienced the same attacks from the devil that we do. Jesus knew everything that was about to happen to Him, but He overcame the spirit of fear, and we can too.

Good Fear and Bad Fear

There is a good fear. There is a normal, healthy fear that God gives us for good in our lives. Here is how you can know the difference between good (healthy) fear and bad (demonic) fear.

JESUS EXPERIENCED THE SAME ATTACKS FROM THE DEVIL THAT WE DO.

Good Fear Is Circumstantial. Bad Fear Is Perpetual.

Imagine the feeling you would have if you were driving down the street and suddenly saw a car coming straight at you. Fear would make you quickly swerve away to save your life and the lives of the other passengers in your car. That fear was not there before the situation happened, and it goes away after the situation ends. That is circumstantial fear; that is good fear.

Bad fear, however, is perpetual; it is a *spirit* of fear. It forces you to live with an abiding sense of anxiety that something bad is about to happen to you. "The other shoe is going to drop." "I am going to go broke." "I am going to die." "There will be a terrorist attack." No matter the situation, the fear remains. Anxiety wears us out and causes us to become depressed. Your emotions cannot handle long-term anxiety without devastating consequences. God never uses the spirit of fear in our lives because we cannot function that way. We are not designed to live like that.

Good Fear Is Protective. Bad Fear Is Paralyzing.

One day, when I was about six years old, my dad and I were walking down the street. We had just moved into our new house, so we didn't know the neighbors or the neighborhood. Out of the corner of my eye, I saw a large dog heading for me as we came to the first street corner. This dog (I later learned his name was Lucky) was apparently very protective of his yard.

Now there was a street sign right on the edge of that yard, and before I knew it, I was on top of that sign. Not just part of the way up—all the way up at the top, above the street names. My dad got between me and Lucky and helped me get down, which I was unable to do by myself. In fact, I later tried several times to climb that sign but could not do it. That is my personal example of protective fear, just like you hear about little ladies picking up the end of a car to free someone underneath.

That is good fear. It is there to protect you. But bad fear is paralyzing. It does not help you get out of trouble; it keeps you in trouble. Have you ever had a dream in which someone was chasing you, and you could not get away? You needed to move, but you were frozen. That is what demonic fear does. It keeps you paralyzed, unable to do good.

Good Fear Is Instructive. Bad Fear Is Confusing.

Good fear is instructive; it tells you when to stop, move, swerve, etc. It says, "Do this, and things will be better for you," and it turns out that way.

Bad fear, on the other hand, is confusing and fatalistic. A spirit of fear is a prophet spirit that tells you your future will be bad for you. It says you will go broke, you will never make it in relationships, people will never like you, and you will die. Demonic fear tells you the exact opposite of what God says in Jeremiah 29:11: "For I know the thoughts that I think toward you, says the Lord, thoughts of peace and not of evil, to give you a future and a hope."

DEMONIC FEAR KEEPS YOU PARALYZED, UNABLE TO DO GOOD.

God has a *good* plan for your future. He will never prophesy gloom and turmoil to control your life. Only the devil does those kinds of things.

Good Fear Is Empowering. Bad Fear Is Enslaving.

Satan uses fear. He tried to use fear in the Garden of Gethsemane to enslave Jesus and prevent Him from accomplishing His purpose. Many believers can be at least partial slaves of fear. Are there things God wants you to do that you think you cannot do because a spirit of fear says you cannot? Satan uses fear because it is all he has to use.

Jesus, on the other hand, is the Prince of Peace (Isaiah 9:6). In John 14:27 He says, "My peace I give to you; not as the world gives do I give to you." Why does Jesus use peace? He is full of it. He thinks peaceful thoughts, He feels peaceful feelings, and He is controlled by peace. Therefore, He leads with peace. You feel peace every time you are being led by God. Colossians 3:15 says, "Let the peace of God rule in your hearts." Don't be ruled by fear. Be ruled by peace.

———

As much as you recognize God's presence by peace, you can recognize Satan's presence by fear. Satan is a defeated foe sentenced to hell, and he knows it. Jesus' triumph over death and sin made a public spectacle of Satan, and now the enemy is full of fear because he knows he has lost. He feels fear, thinks fear, and is controlled by fear; he wants us to be the same way. *When you feel fear, you are feeling the presence of the devil.* I am not saying you are of the devil; Satan simply tries to attack all of us.

The devil is not a gentleman. On your weakest day, when you are struggling and confused, he will attack you. He will attack children, the elderly, the sick, and the hurting. He does not care—he is evil through and through. Therefore, when you sense fear in your life, understand that the devil is trying to control you the way he is controlled. But also remember that Jesus is your Prince of Peace.

How to Overcome Fear

Admit Your Fear Without Shame

I noted Luke's account above, and you also can read the story in Matthew 26:36–46 and Mark 14:32–42. Jesus took His disciples and brought them into the Garden of Gethsemane. Then He took Peter, James, and John further into the garden and poured out His heart: *I am dying. I am unbelievably upset right now, guys. Would you please pray with me?* Then He turned, got down on His knees, and said, "Abba, Father." Abba means "daddy." Jesus said, *Daddy, I am scared. I do not want to die on the cross. I do not want to do this. If there is any way, Daddy, will You let me out of this situation?* He prayed it three times. Jesus admitted His fear without shame.

We all feel fear. Growing up, I felt fear all the time, but I did not know how to deal with it. Even when I was a

JESUS ADMITTED HIS FEAR WITHOUT SHAME.

young man, I did not know how to deal with fear. After all, I was a young *man*. Little girls or young ladies get to cry, scream, and do things like that. But a young man would be called a "sissy" for doing that. Men do not get to cry and scream; you just take it. You just be a "man."

When I was fearful, I learned to assume the "stance": chest out, chin out, and sending the message, "Come on! Get over here with your bad self. Grab all you think you can ride, and I will give you some." On the inside, though, I was hoping, "Oh, please don't!" I did not know any better; that was just the way I responded. The more afraid I felt, the more macho I got. But the truth is that it does not work. I eventually got to a place in the Lord where I realized that it is okay to say I am afraid.

Many times we fight in our marriages because of fear. We really do. When you are fighting with your spouse, most often you are fighting about your fears. We fear not being protected, not being provided for, and not being accepted. And because we are afraid, we begin to fight and act tough, rather than humbly admitting our fears and bringing them out into the light.

The spirit of fear wants to stay in darkness because Satan is the prince of darkness. Anything in the darkness is under his domain. You cannot kick the devil off his own property. The only thing you can do is take fear and bring it into the light. Jesus is full of light.

There is something incredibly healing and powerful about simply saying, "I am afraid, and I am not ashamed of it. I am just a human being. This is way beyond me,

WHEN YOU SUBMIT YOUR FEAR TO GOD, FEAR NO LONGER TELLS YOU WHAT TO DO.

and I am not going to act tough and confident because I do not feel tough and confident. I feel very fearful."

Jesus understands, and He is merciful about our fears. Feeling fear does not mean there is something wrong with us. I feel fear all the time about many things. I just have to bring it into the light. I need to talk to Karen or my close friends about it, and I need to talk to God about it.

Submit Your Fear to God

Jesus came into the garden and said, *Father, I am afraid. Daddy, I do not want to die like this. Please take this cup away.* He also said, "Not My will, but Yours, be done" (Luke 22:42). That is what it means to submit your fear to God. Your feelings are not your master—God is. You may feel afraid, but you choose not to act on your feelings.

When you submit your fear to God, fear no longer tells you what to do. You may feel like running away, but you will not do anything unless God tells you to do it. God's Word directs your life.

I lived many years of my life making most of my decisions based on fear. I will tell you that I regret every decision I have ever made by fear, and no decision I have made by fear has turned out right. I have never made a decision based on fear that made me later think, "Thank God I made that decision. That was the right choice."

If you want to starve a monster, do not feed it. If you want to make a monster bigger, just keep feeding it. The more decisions you make by fear, the bigger the spirit gets, and the more it controls your life.

Just because we feel something does not make it true. Just because our emotions are real do not mean they are *right*. For many of us, the greatest regrets that we have in our lives are things we did when we were feeling something real. The lust, the greed, the hate, the self-hate ... whatever it might have been, it was real, but it was not right

Jesus came to His Father and said, *Father, this is real.* Jesus was born and sent for a purpose, but He did not want to do it. *This is real, Father, but You will tell me what is right.*

We need to learn how to live not by our emotions but by God and His word. The more you act upon faith and what God says, the freer you will be, and the more your life will turn out for good. But the more you do what your emotions say, especially when your emotions are working against the Word of God, the more you will regret your actions. As I said before, I have made many decisions based on fear. I regret every single one of them.

Focus on God's Presence and Love

I love Luke 22:44: "And being in agony, He prayed more earnestly." The more Jesus hurt, the more He prayed. He kept His eyes on God.

In Psalm 23:4 King David declares,

> Yea, though I walk through the valley of shadow of death,
> I will fear no evil;
> For you *are* with me;
> Your rod and Your staff, they comfort me.

THE MORE JESUS HURT, THE MORE HE PRAYED. HE KEPT HIS EYES ON GOD.

David says, *I am going through a near-death experience, but because I keep my eyes on You, I do not have any fear.*

How did Jesus overcome fear? He quoted Scripture to Himself on the way to the cross.

> I have set the Lord always before me;
> Because *He is* at my right hand I shall not be moved.
> Therefore my heart is glad, and my glory rejoices;
> My flesh also will rest in hope.
> For You will not leave my soul in Sheol,
> Nor will You allow Your Holy One to see corruption.
> You will show me the path of life;
> In Your presence *is* fullness of joy;
> At Your right hand *are* pleasures forevermore
> (Psalm 16:8–11).

When Satan attacked Jesus in the Garden of Gethsemane, he probably said things like, "Ready to die, Jesus? Are You really ready to die? Because death is my domain. I am going to kill You, drag You to hell, and keep You there forever. No one will ever rescue You. I am the prince of death, and no one has ever been rescued from my grasp."

While Satan was telling Jesus these lies, Jesus declared, *I have set the Lord always before me. I am not setting Satan and all of his lies before me. I will not focus on what he is saying to me right now. Father, You will not let my body rot in the ground. You will not leave me in hell. In Your presence there is fullness of joy, and at Your right hand there are pleasures forevermore. I am not staying down there!* That is how Jesus made it.

The devil wants to take the spirit of fear and wave death in your face. He wants to rub your nose in it until you lie down and die or turn around and run the other way. But God is with us. As we read in the last chapter, Hebrews 13:5 promises that God is *always* with us. Verse 6 says,

> "The Lord *is* my helper;
> I will not fear.
> What can man do to me?"

God will never leave you; He will never forsake you. Even if you do not feel like He is with you, He *is* there. When you focus your life on God, you will be full of courage. Courage is not the absence of fear. Courage is doing the right thing in the presence of fear. When you put your eyes on God, He will give you the courage to do the right thing.

Face Your Fears by Faith and Watch Them Crumble

Jesus prayed three times, "Let this cup pass from Me" (Matthew 26:39–44). Then He looked up and saw the torches of those coming to arrest Him, with Judas leading the crowd. Jesus had His answer.

He did not run, though. The disciples ran, but Jesus stood His ground. He went to the cross, suffered, and died. After His resurrection, Jesus' first words to the disciples were, "Peace to you" (Luke 24:36). *Peace.* Jesus felt fear, but He faced His fear by faith, and He will never have fear again. He is full of peace.

Sometimes God will deliver you from your fears, but much of the time God delivers us *in* our fears. Sometimes you just have to face your fears. You may be afraid of rejection, intimacy, being vulnerable, or loving people. But God wants you to love people. And in the midst of loving people, He will set you free.

Perhaps you fear poverty. You want to prosper, but you are afraid. God wants you to give, and in giving you will learn to be free.

God does not place us in environments where we never have to face our fears. Sometimes you have to run toward the roar to kill the lion.

One day, I got on an airplane, and sitting across from me was a young woman, probably 25 or 30 years old. This woman was absolutely terrified of flying. She had friends sitting right next to her, and these friends were trying to comfort her. We were still sitting at the gate when she grabbed the first airsick bag and started throwing up. The plane had not moved an inch, and she was already sick from fear. She suffered through the entire flight like that.

Some fears in life may be like that. Face up to them. The first time you may be like that young woman, needing three airsick bags to make it through the flight. That is alright. The next time you will need just two. The third time you will need just one. And then you will not need any at all. After you have flown a dozen times, you will be sleeping on the airplane. You will not be afraid anymore.

SOMETIMES GOD WILL DELIVER YOU FROM YOUR FEARS, BUT MUCH OF THE TIME GOD DELIVERS US IN OUR FEARS.

Satan wants you to live your life in fear so that you are paralyzed and cannot do what God wants you to do. Sometimes God will deliver us from our fears, but more often He will tell you to stand up and run to the roar. He will say, *Stop letting that demon control your life. By faith do what I am telling you to do, and I will rescue you.*

———————

Jesus did not run from the cross. He went willingly, and He died on it. When He was resurrected, He came to His disciples and said, "Peace." The fear was gone. It was there for a moment, but God was with Jesus. Jesus faced His fear, and now He gives peace to you and me.

Many of the things I was terrified of earlier in my life no longer frighten me today. God did not deliver me from them, but He delivered me in them. I had to turn and begin to do things that scared me. If we face our fears, "the peace of God, which surpasses all understanding, will guard [our] hearts and minds through Christ Jesus" (Philippians 4:7).

3

OVERCOMING COMPARISON

THERE IS A good kind of a comparison. Sometimes we can be inspired and educated by comparison, like when we see the way another person loves their spouse or how another couple parents their children. We see that we can do better, and we can learn from their example. That is a good kind of comparison.

However, the kind of comparison I am talking about in this chapter is the type that the devil uses to implant negative thoughts about God, ourselves, and others in our minds. This is a common ploy, and it can cause us to do things that keep us from being the people God wants us to be.

The story in the final chapter of the Gospel of John is an interesting example of comparison. Jesus has already died and been resurrected, and now He is about to ascend into heaven. This is the third time He has appeared to His disciples after the resurrection. The "disciple whom Jesus loved" in this account refers to John, the writer of this Gospel.

> When they had eaten breakfast, Jesus said to Simon Peter, "Simon, *son* of Jonah, do you love Me more than these?"

He said to Him, "Yes, Lord; You know that I love You."

He said to him, "Feed My lambs."

He said to him again a second time, "Simon, *son* of Jonah, do you love Me?"

He said to Him, "Yes, Lord; You know that I love You."

He said to him, "Tend My sheep."

He said to him the third time, "Simon, *son* of Jonah, do you love Me?" Peter was grieved because He said to him the third time, "Do you love Me?"

And he said to Him, "Lord, You know all things; You know that I love You."

Jesus said to him, "Feed My sheep. Most assuredly, I say to you, when you were younger, you girded yourself and walked where you wished; but when you are old, you will stretch out your hands, and another will gird you and carry *you* where you do not wish." This He spoke, signifying by what death he would glorify God. And when He had spoken this, He said to him, "Follow Me."

Then Peter, turning around, saw the disciple whom Jesus loved following, who also had leaned on His breast at the supper, and said, "Lord, who is the one who betrays You?" Peter, seeing him, said to Jesus, "But Lord, what *about* this man?"

Jesus said to him, "If I will that he remain till I come, what *is that* to you? You follow Me" (John 21:15–22).

Just days earlier, Peter had openly denied Jesus. Jesus had warned him, "Before the rooster crows, you will deny Me three times" (Matthew 26:34). And even though Peter had vowed not to, he did just that. This event had not yet been resolved, so Jesus chose this setting by the Sea of Tiberias to do so.

Jesus says to Peter, "Do you love Me? ... Feed My sheep." He is establishing Peter as the preeminent apostle in the midst of the other disciples and restoring him back into ministry. Jesus establishes *love* as the only legitimate basis of serving and following Him. Loving Jesus first and foremost is the most important qualification for ministry. Why? Loving Jesus causes us to love people, but loving people doesn't necessarily cause us to love God. God must always be first (see Matthew 22:37–39).

As He is restoring Peter, Jesus does something shocking: He tells Peter how he will die. In verse 18 Jesus says that when Peter gets older, people will bind him and take him where he does not want to go. Church history records the fulfillment of this prophecy many years later when Peter is sentenced to die via crucifixion according to the Roman tradition. However, the apostle declared, "I am not worthy to be crucified like my Lord," so they crucified him upside down instead. That is why you will sometimes see an upside-down cross in Saint Peter's churches or in St. Peter's Basilica.

Why does Jesus tell Peter how he is going to die? I believe one reason is that this disciple had been a coward. The threat of martyrdom is what caused Peter to deny Jesus in the first place, and Jesus wants him to understand the cost of taking on the responsibility of sharing the gospel. Jesus says, *Peter, you have to settle this issue. If you follow Me, your life will end in martyrdom. I want you to know that up front.*

LOVING JESUS FIRST AND FOREMOST IS THE MOST IMPORTANT QUALIFICATION FOR MINISTRY.

I believe the other reason Jesus makes this revelation is to settle Peter's problem with insecurity and comparison. Luke 22:24–27 records the argument the disciples had at the Last Supper about which one of them was the greatest. This was a frequent debate among those men. James and John even asked Jesus to let them sit on either side of Him when He came into glory, much to the other disciples' resentment. The disciples constantly fought for position, a struggle that is always based in insecurity. You never feel the need to scramble to the top when you are feeling secure.

Jesus had twelve disciples, but Peter, James, and John were especially close to Him. These three shared special experiences with Jesus that no other disciples did, such as witnessing Jesus' transformation on the mountain (Matthew 17:1–13), the healing of Jairus' daughter (Mark 5:37–43), and Jesus' prayer in the Garden of Gethsemane (Matthew 26:36–42).

Peter and John likely felt some rivalry, each wanting to be the *greatest* follower of Jesus. So when Jesus tells Peter he is going to die a terrible death, Peter immediately turns toward John and asks, "But Lord, what *about* this man?" (John 21:21). His meaning is obvious: "Jesus, encourage me by telling me that John is going to die like me or even worse."

If we are honest with ourselves, we must admit that we are all like that. We are obsessed with how we compare to others at all times. We are happiest when we are equal to or greater than others, and we are the most miserable when we are less than others in any significant way.

Peter certainly wants to hear that John will suffer as much himself, but that is not what Jesus says. To Peter's "What *about* this man?" Jesus replies, "If I will that he remain till I come, what *is that* to you? You follow Me." Jesus is not promising that John will live forever. He is simply telling Peter that his role is to follow Jesus, not worry about anyone else.

Jesus has no sympathy with comparison. His response to Peter is the same response He gives to us: "You follow Me." Peter could not accomplish his mission of sharing the gospel if he was focused on comparing himself with others, and neither can we.

The Curse of Comparison

Unhealthy comparison makes us insecure, miserable, competitive, gossipy, and bitter. It produces thoughts and feelings about God, ourselves, and others that are inaccurate, counterproductive, and even destructive. Comparison is a *curse* on our lives.

Comparison Produces Arrogance and Insecurity

Comparison can produce feelings of both arrogance (superiority) and insecurity (inferiority).When you compare yourself with other people, you may think that you are better than them, which leads to pride, or you may feel like they are better than you, which leads to insecurity.

CONSTANT COMPARISON WITH OTHERS WILL ALWAYS BEAT YOU DOWN.

I believe comparison is one of the top reasons for insecurity. Many years ago I read a statistic which said that more than 90 percent of fashion models have very low self-esteem. Out of all groups of people, you would think that beautiful women who make their living as fashion models would probably have tremendous self-esteem. So why do they have such low self-esteem? Because they are endlessly compared with other women. Constant comparison with others will always beat you down.

Comparison Keeps Us Focused on People Rather than God

Comparison keeps me focused on myself and others rather than focusing on God. That is why Jesus says to Peter, "You follow Me." In other words, *Get your eyes off John.* When I am constantly comparing, I am not following Jesus. I cannot be focused on Him when I am vigilantly comparing myself to everybody else. Romans 8:5–6 says,

> For those who live according to the flesh set their minds on the things of the flesh, but those *who live* according to the Spirit, the things of the Spirit. For to be carnally minded *is* death, but to be spiritually minded *is* life and peace.

Comparison Hinders Our Trust in God

It may be at a subconscious level, but comparison keeps us mistrustful of God and offended at Him. Like Peter, we begin to compare ourselves with others. What about people who are richer or better looking than you?

What about those who are smarter, happier, or have better marriages? There will always be someone who seems to have everything better than you do.

If you are not careful, comparison will not only create a barrier between you and other people, but it will also plant seeds of mistrust and offense against God. Comparison made Peter think, "Does Jesus love John more than He loves me? Why would He have me martyred but let John live forever?" This is the kernel of mistrust that the devil uses to separate us from God.

Rejection of who God has made us to be is the root of comparison. Here is a very important truth: something will never be right in our relationship with God, and we will never be free, until we sincerely thank Him for who we are, what we are, and where we are. Comparison makes us believe that God loves other people more than He loves us, and that is not true at all. We are *all* His favorites.

Comparison Makes Us Resentful and Rejecting of Others

Comparison causes us to be resentful and rejecting of others who have what we want. Some of the people we resent the most have only done one thing wrong—they have what we want.

Many years ago, I counseled a couple in our church who were struggling financially. Frankly, the husband was lazy and did not want to work, so the wife had to take on the burden of the finances herself. They were part of a life group that was hosted by a godly couple

REJECTION OF WHO GOD HAS MADE US TO BE IS THE ROOT OF COMPARISON.

who were financially well-off. During this time, the host couple sold their house, built a new home, and moved.

When the host couple moved into their new home, the struggling couple just went crazy. They were extremely offended at the host couple and actually left the church over it. They came to see me before leaving, and the wife ranted, "I just cannot believe that they have all this money! They could give this money to the church, and they should not be building this new house!" I let her vent her frustrations, and then I replied, "I am so sorry for your financial struggles. To be honest, though, the only thing they have done wrong is they have what you want. You wish that you had the same affluence they do, and you want a home like they have."

If we cannot accept or celebrate other people's blessings, there is something wrong with us—not with them.

Comparison Makes Us Try to Be Something We Are Not

Comparison makes us try to be something we are not in order to measure up and feel good about ourselves. However, the surest way to fail is to try to change an unchangeable, and the unchangeable is you. You can only be you; you cannot be someone else. Every person has a unique calling and destiny. If you feel like you *have* to be a doctor, a lawyer, a millionaire, or a superstar to measure up, you will never be happy. In other words, God created you to be you, so the only thing you can succeed at is being you. Peter had to be Peter, and John had to be John. They both had to be themselves.

GOD CREATED YOU TO BE YOU, SO THE ONLY THING YOU CAN SUCCEED AT IS BEING YOU.

God loves all of us equally, but this love is expressed in different ways. He loves all of us according to the unique plan He has for each of our lives. Psalm 139:16 says, "In Your book, they all were written, / The days fashioned for me, / When *as yet there were* none of them." Focusing on comparison and trying to be something you are not can abort God's plan for your life.

Comparison Is an Open Door for the Devil to Work

James 3:14–16 says,

> If you have bitter envy and self-seeking in your hearts, do not boast and lie against the truth. This wisdom does not descend from above, but *is* earthly, sensual, demonic. For where envy and self-seeking *exist,* confusion and every evil thing *are* there.

Envy is the basis of almost all comparison. The definition of envy is a feeling of discontent or covetousness regarding another person's advantages, success, possessions, etc. Psalm 106:16 says that the children of Israel rebelled against Moses because of envy. Matthew 27:18 says that the Jews turned Jesus over to the Romans because of envy. Envy says, "I do not like it that you are better off than me. I do not like it that you have more power than me."

Envy is a boundary violation. It refuses to recognize God's sovereign right to parent and bless as He pleases. It refuses to allow Him to do for someone else what He hasn't done for us.

When you have to pull another person down to bring yourself up, that is not God—that is the devil. James 3 says that where self-seeking and envy exist, there is disorder and evil at work. If I have to pull others down to bring myself up, then two things are certain: God is not my source, and I cannot say that the fruit of the Holy Spirit is evident in my life.

Envy and comparison create an open door for the devil to come in and work in our lives. We become different kinds of people when we are under the influence of envy. Do you struggle with envy? To find out, ask yourself one question: "Can I rejoice with those more blessed than I am in an area?"

Considerations Concerning Comparison

Here are some important points to consider that will help us put negative comparison in right perspective.

Nobody Gets the Whole Package

In 1 Corinthians 12:12 the apostle Paul writes,

> For as the body is one and has many members, but all the members of that one body, being many, are one body, so also *is* Christ. For by one Spirit we were all baptized into one body.

As members of the body of Christ, we are all part of the package, but not one of us has the whole package. Some of us are eyes, ears, hands, or toes—whatever God has gifted and blessed us to be. To the degree we are gifted or endowed in one area, we are very ungifted and un-endowed in others. If you want to be somebody

else, remember that according to the Bible, we are
a body.

The Greater a Person's Influence, the Less Their Impact

We tend to desire influence over impact, even though
impact is more common and even more necessary. For
example, a teacher has influence on more children
than an individual mother does, but a mother has more
impact on her children than the children's teacher
does. The President of the United States will have more
influence on all Americans, but the mayor of your city
will have more impact on you personally. Evangelists,
such as myself, will influence thousands, if not millions,
of people around the world through television and
books. However, we will not impact people as directly or
profoundly as their pastors, group leaders, and friends.

Do not give up impact for influence when God has
called you to impact. We often compare ourselves to
those who have a big platform, but people who have
a small circle of influence actually have the greatest
impact on the lives of others.

God Places the Most Profound Giftings in the People and Places We Least Expect

Paul continues in 1 Corinthians 12,

> Those *members* of the body which we think to be less
> honorable, on these we bestow greater honor; and our
> unpresentable *parts* have greater modesty, but our
> presentable *parts* have no need. But God composed the
> body, having given greater honor to that *part* which lacks

it, that there should be no schism in the body, but *that* the members should have the same care for one another (vv. 23–25).

Within the Church we often think that the greatest gifts are on the platform when, in fact, they are actually in the audience. God does not want the Church to have a hierarchy like the world has. Instead, He designed the body of Christ in such a way that we will not succeed without honoring and accepting every individual as gifted and important. God gives different giftings to us to so that we can honor and minister to each other.

God overlooks no one. Whenever you feel as if you want to be another person or have their giftings, remember that you *are* significant in the body of Christ.

The Greater the Responsibility, Influence, or Authority, the Greater the Stress

Many people dream of being Billy Graham, the president of the United States, a major league sports star, or the CEO of a multi-billion dollar company. They fail to realize, however, that such increased responsibility, influence, and authority come with much higher levels of stress. Stress neutralizes the satisfaction of everything we do. Instead of enjoying their elite circumstances, many people in high-stress positions envy those in lower-stress positions.

We All Deal with Insecurity

Did you know that we often feel insecure at the same time as others? Four or five people may be standing in a group, and each one may be thinking something different.

- "I wish I had her body."
- "I wish I had his friends."
- "I wish I had their house."
- "I wish I had their marriage."

Everyone feels insecure about something, and our insecurities fuel virtually all comparison.

Everyone Has Pain

We often objectify people and look at them in a one-dimensional manner. We judge others on how they look, what they drive, where they live, and how much money they make. The problem is that everyone—yes, *everyone*—has pain. We just don't see it because pain is often a private, hidden issue.

When I was a member at my local YMCA, I met the man who had the locker next to mine. I did not know he was very wealthy, but we struck up a friendship and talked occasionally. It was only later that I found out how wealthy he was.

One day I asked this man how he was doing and where he had been lately (I had not seen him for a while). He replied that he had been traveling around the country looking for his daughter. I was surprised to learn that his daughter had schizophrenia. She was an adult, maybe 30 or 40 years old at the time. He said that she lived on the streets, and he would find her in different places like Seattle, Chicago, or Los Angeles. He would find her, get

EVERYONE FEELS INSECURE ABOUT SOMETHING, AND OUR INSECURITIES FUEL VIRTUALLY ALL COMPARISON.

her into care, but then she would always get back on the street. This man spent most of his time looking for his daughter. He said, "I do not want her to die on the street. I want her to receive the care that she needs."

Most people would look at this man, see only his wealth and position, and think, "I wish I was like him." They would have no idea that he experienced such pain.

I saw a lady on TV one time who was on a special about breast cancer. Her grandmother, mother, and sisters had all died of breast cancer. This woman did not currently have breast cancer, but she carried the breast cancer gene, and she had daughters who likely carried the gene as well.

This woman was very beautiful—the type who would walk down the street and be admired by both men and women for her figure. However, she did not see her body as something admirable; rather, this woman said her breasts were time bombs that would eventually kill herself and every woman in her family. The very thing that other people envied and objectified about this woman brought her pain.

We must understand that regardless of how good or godly people are, everybody has pain. And you cannot have what they have unless you take the pain that comes with it. Jesus had pain, so Peter had pain too.

Which disciple would you rather be: Peter or John? Jesus tells Peter that he will die a bad death. Peter looks at John and says, *What about that man?* Jesus responds by asking why it matters to Peter if John lives forever. The other disciples took this to mean that John would not have pain. However, this was not the case at all. John did outlive the other disciples, all of whom were martyred. However, he was also exiled as a political prisoner to the island of Patmos, where he likely died alone of old age.

Would you rather die in action as a martyr or die alone of old age as an exiled prisoner? The pains of loneliness and martyrdom may actually be pretty close, but the point is that both Peter and John had pain. Everybody has pain.

Greater Blessings and Giftings Produce Greater Accountability with God

In Luke 12:48 Jesus says, "For everyone to whom much is given, from him much will be required; and to whom much has been committed, of him they will ask the more." When we compare ourselves to others who are more blessed or gifted in particular areas, we often fail to remember that the required accountability for those areas is greater as well. This is especially true for those who hold positions of authority in the Church. James 3:1 says, "My brethren, let not many of you become teachers, knowing that we shall receive a stricter judgment."

Causes of Comparison

As we look at the different causes of comparison, I encourage you to ask the Holy Spirit, "Do I struggle with any of these?"

1. **Lack of acceptance in who God made me to be**
    - Matthew 22:39 says, "You shall love your neighbor as yourself."
    - Self-love is biblical and crucial to our relationship with God and others.

2. **Lack of security and identity in God**
    - We often search for temporal and external means of security.
    - Are you basing your identity on your position, status, or others' acceptance?
    - Jeremiah 17:7 promises blessings for those who trust and hope in the Lord.

3. **Greed**
    - The definition of *greed* is "excessive desire."
    - Greed always wants more than we need and more than God wants us to have.
    - An orphan spirit has to have too much to be enough.
    - An entitlement spirit believes it has the right to have what it wants and what others have as well.

4. **Wrong concept of God**
    - Do you interpret God's "greater blessings" upon others or advantages others have as a sign of His preference or greater love?
    - Do you feel rejected when you witness others being blessed?

5. **Lack of love for others**
    - Why did Peter want to know that John was going to suffer too? Peter dealt with pettiness and lack of love.

ARE YOU BASING YOUR IDENTITY ON YOUR POSITION, STATUS, OR OTHERS' ACCEPTANCE?

- If you really love someone, you want something good for them. If you don't love them, you resent them when something good happens to them.

6. **Covetousness**

   - The definition of *covet* is to desire wrongfully, inordinately, or without due regard for the rights of others.
   - Covetousness refuses to allow others to have the things we can't have.
   - It is rooted in not trusting God to care for us and give us what we need.
   - Covetousness causes pettiness and rejection.

7. **Jealousy and envy**

   - *Jealousy* is feeling resentment against someone because of that person's rivalry, success, or advantages.
   - *Envy* is a feeling of discontent or covetousness with regard to another's advantages, success, possessions, etc.
   - Jealousy is usually about people. Envy is usually about things.
   - 1 John 2:15–16 says, "Do not love the world or the things in the world. If anyone loves the world, the love of the Father is not in him. For all that *is* in the world—the lust of the flesh, the lust of the eyes, and the pride of life—is not of the Father but is of the world."

How to Overcome Comparison

Now that we understand the causes and consequences of comparison, we can focus on how to become overcomers in this area.

Thank God for Who You Are and Accept Yourself

Rejecting who we are in God is the number one reason that we compare. Do you ever think, "I am just not that special. I just do not measure up."? Let me tell you something: God made you in your mother's womb, and you are fearfully and wonderfully made. You are unique in God.

The devil will beat you up for the rest of your life until you choose to wake up every morning and say, "God, thank You for who You made me to be. Thank You for what You made me to do. Thank You for placing me in the exact place You want me to be." When you start feeling insecure, and the devil tempts you to compare yourself with others, just praise God. You are special in the Lord.

Trust God with Your Needs and Desires

Instead of focusing on others, focus on being the person God wants you to be. Trust Him to make you into the person you want to become.

We do not want to have to drag other people down to pull ourselves up. We can *all* get everything that God wants us to have, and all be okay. I know my Daddy will take care of me, and I hope He blesses you at the same time.

REJECTING WHO WE ARE IN GOD IS THE NUMBER ONE REASON THAT WE COMPARE.

If you do not trust God for favor and opportunity, you will take matters into your own hands. You will become competitive, jealous, envious, and covetous. You will not have good relationships.

God can get you where *He* wants you to go. When Jesus told Peter about his future, the disciple should have said, "I accept it," instead of comparing himself to anyone else. Peter struggled to accept who God made him to be because he wanted to be equal to or greater than everybody else around him. We are all equal in God, but we are also all different in God. We need to put our eyes on God and keep them off people.

Trust God's Work in Other People

We need to stop interfering with God's work in other people's lives. Comparison leads to manipulation, gossip, and tearing others down. For example, when someone gets a new car or a promotion, we start talking negatively about them. Even within our own group of friends, we secretly try to manipulate relationships and situations to ensure that no one gets an advantage over us. If they do, we start hacking away at the ladder on which they are standing.

This is a vitally important concept to grasp: if you do not let God be God in other people's lives, He will not be God for you. If you do not let God bless other people the way He wants to bless them, He will not bless you the way you want Him to bless you. God is fair and just, and He loves all of us the same amount—just not in the same way. We must let God be God.

Be a Giver and Encourager

We must learn to bless others and celebrate their advantages. Romans 12:15 says, "Rejoice with those who rejoice, and weep with those who weep." I want to be the kind of person who helps others prosper and achieve. I want to be able to say, "Even if I can't have something, I'm glad you can have it."

––––––––––

Ask God to help you take your eyes off others and keep them on Jesus. Surrender to being who God has made you to be. That is the only way to overcome comparison.

4

OVERCOMING SHAME

Since we are surrounded by so great a cloud of witnesses,
let us lay aside every weight, and the sin which so easily
ensnares *us,* and let us run with endurance the race that is set
before us, looking unto Jesus, the author and finisher of
our faith, who for the joy that was set before Him endured
the cross, despising the shame, and has sat down at
the right hand of the throne of God.

—Hebrews 12:1–2

WHEN JESUS WAS arrested and sentenced to death by crucifixion, the guards stripped Him naked. They beat Him, slapped Him, and spit on Him. They did every humiliating thing you can do to a human being, and then they hung Jesus naked just outside Jerusalem. Long before air travel, this area was the crossroads of Africa, Europe, Asia, and the Middle East. Like Grand Central Station, it was the center of the known world.

Jesus hung on a cross with a sign above His head that said, "The King of the Jews" (Mark 15:26). During His years of ministry, Jesus had openly claimed to be the Son of God. Hanging on the cross, He looked like a big failure. He was shame personified.

Incredibly, though, the writer of Hebrews says that Jesus despised the shame. The English word *despise* is derived from the Greek word *kataphronesas*. This word comes from *kata,* which means "from" or "away," and *phreneao*, which means "thinking" or "mind."

Kataphronesas literally means "to think nothing"—not allowing a thought into your mind. As Jesus hung on the cross, Satan relentlessly attacked Him with thoughts of shame: "You are a failure; you are no good. What an embarrassment you are to your family. What an embarrassment you are to the Jewish race. What an embarrassment you are to your Father."

Of course, everything in the natural seemed to line up with what Satan was saying. However, Jesus would not let any of those thoughts into His mind. He refused to think thoughts of shame even as He suffered and died the most excruciating death imaginable.

Jesus completely and eternally defeated shame on the cross, and He defeated it for us too. We can live our lives successfully without any shame whatsoever. In fact, we can only live the lives God wants us to live if we are free from shame. We must be free from shame to be able to do what God wants us to do.

Understanding Shame

To understand shame, I want to give you a biblical zoology lesson. I want to talk to you about three important animals related to shame in the Bible.

JESUS COMPLETELY AND ETERNALLY DEFEATED SHAME ON THE CROSS, AND HE DEFEATED IT FOR US TOO.

The Serpent

The first animal is the serpent in the Garden of Eden, which is very important because this is where shame originally came from. Referring to Adam and Eve, Genesis 2:25 says, "They were both naked, the man and his wife, and were not ashamed."

God creates you to be shameless. He never has and never will use shame in your life. Why? Because God cannot function in an atmosphere of shame. He cannot do what He wants to do in our lives when shame is present. That is why everything that God creates and everything that God controls is shameless. The paradise God created in the Garden of Eden was designed for shameless living.

So where did shame come from? In Genesis 3 the devil takes on the form of a serpent and tempts Eve to eat from the tree of the knowledge of good and evil. This is the only tree in the entire garden that God has told Adam and Even not to eat from, but Eve gives in to temptation.

> So when the woman saw that the tree *was* good for food, that it *was* pleasant to the eyes, and a tree desirable to make *one* wise, she took of its fruit and ate. She also gave to her husband with her, and he ate. Then the eyes of both of them were opened, and they knew that they *were* naked (Genesis 3:6–7a).

Sin opened the door for Satan to whisper a lie into Adam and Eve's souls that would change the human race from that point forward. The lie was that their nakedness was perverted and wrong. That is why they hid from each other and from God. The very first symptom of sin in the human race was shame.

The Scripture continues,

> They knew that they *were* naked; and they sewed fig leaves together and made themselves coverings.
>
> And they heard the sound of the Lord God walking in the garden in the cool of the day, and Adam and his wife hid themselves from the presence of the Lord God among the trees of the garden.
>
> Then the Lord God called to Adam and said to him, "Where *are* you?"
>
> So he said, "I heard Your voice in the garden, and I was afraid because I was naked; and I hid myself."
>
> And He said, "Who told you that you *were* naked? Have you eaten from the tree of which I commanded you that you should not eat?" (Genesis 3:7b–11).

Satan comes into the garden and does what Satan does—he advertises. He tries to make Adam and Eve believe that sin is the answer, and the instant they do sin, he ministers shame. Sin is the problem, but shame is the symptom.

Remember, Satan is the hurt whisperer. We may not always recognize that it is him, but every time there is a sin, a failure, a trauma, or a problem in your life, you can count on the devil to be there to interpret reality to you at that moment.

The devil does not announce himself. He is stealthy; after all, he is a serpent. That is why God asks a hiding, shame-filled Adam, *Who told you that you were naked?* God never asks a question to get the answer. He asks a question so that we will get the answer. Adam and Eve are completely unaware of the fact that the moment they sinned, they opened a door for the devil. And the devil immediately began whispering, "You are defective. There is something wrong with you."

God created Adam and Eve naked. There was nothing wrong with their nakedness; it was glorious and pure. It was not nudity like we would think of now; rather, they were covered with the glory of God. God created them perfectly, with no need to hide from each other. But when shame entered the picture, everything changed. Shame causes us to hide from each other and from God.

So who told Adam and Eve they were naked? The serpent did. Shame always comes from the devil because he cannot operate in an atmosphere of shamelessness. There has to be shame for the enemy to do what he wants to do in our lives.

How Shame Changes Us

Shame changes the way we see and think about ourselves.

Before Adam and Eve sinned, they were fine. When they sinned, shame came into the human race and changed the way they saw and thought about themselves. Shame lowered their self-esteem and made them ashamed of who they were.

SHAME CAUSES US TO HIDE FROM EACH OTHER AND FROM GOD.

*Shame changes the way we interact with others
and destroys our potential for relationships.*

Before shame, Adam and Eve were helpmates. They had perfect intimacy and a perfect relationship in the Garden of Eden. After shame, they hid from one another and accused each other.

*Shame changes the way we think about God
and relate to Him.*

Before shame came into the Garden of Eden, Adam and Eve walked with God intimately in the cool of the day. After shame came in, they were afraid of God and hid from Him. Shame changes everything about the human condition.

How to Define Shame

This definition of shame comes from the book *Free Yourself, Be Yourself* by Alan Wright. Previously titled *Shame Off You*, it is the best book on shame I have ever read, and it has ministered to both Karen and myself a great deal.

Alan Wright defines shame as "a feeling of being inwardly flawed—of not measuring up."[1] Shame says, *There is just something wrong with me.*

This is what the devil says to us in trauma, in sin, and in failure. We do not know it is the devil because he does not want us to know it is him. He would rather us believe it is ourselves, or worse yet, God. As soon as we

1. Alan D. Wright, *Free Yourself, Be Yourself* (Colorado Springs: Multnomah, 2010), 18.

sin, the devil slithers up and says, "There is something wrong with you. You are not like most other people. You are no good. You are a failure, and you are always going to be a failure. There is just something not right about you."

Wright also says, "Knowing you have to measure up in order to feel acceptable while knowing that you can't quite measure up leaves you with a gnawing anxiety that wreaks havoc in your soul."[2] Shame says, *God expects certain things of me to be acceptable. Maybe people expect things of me to be acceptable too, and I am stuck here and cannot get any higher.* We cannot bridge the gap between who we think we need to be and who we are, so we feel shame and have to deal with it in some way.

How to Recognize Shame

If someone would have come up to me when I was younger and asked, "Do you have shame in your life?" I would have said no. Karen would have said yes; she had dealt with shame all of her life. But me? I would have said no. I was actually full of shame, but I did not know how to recognize it, and I certainly did not know how to deal with it.

Here are some ways to recognize shame.

1. **Having a fear of exposure and intimacy**
    You are afraid of someone finding out who you really are. This is like the fig leaves for Adam and Eve.

2. Wright, 19.

2. **Never feeling like you do well enough; being driven by performance and perfectionism**
    I have lived most of my life that way.

3. **Being devastated by criticism**
    This is not just being bothered by criticism. After all, nobody *likes* criticism. I am talking about when criticism from others disables you.

4. **Being overly critical of ourselves or others; having extremes of bitterness, rage, compliance, and needing to please people**
    In one day, or even in one hour, we go from being enraged against people who make us feel badly about ourselves to trying to please people.

5. **Being primarily motivated by what other people think**
    This is not simply caring about what others think. This is about your life being *controlled* by what other people think. I once helped a family through a tragedy, and I quickly found out that they did not want anyone to know they had problems. They had worked for years to try to keep their horrific problems hidden because they were so afraid of what other people might think. The fear of shame hindered them from getting the help they needed.

6. **Being primarily motivated by fear (fear of failure or fear of rejection)**
    Again, this is not just having some fear, which is normal. When fear is the driving motivation for what we do, shame is likely involved.

7. **Underperforming to avoid risk**

   Shame says, "I do not want to be successful. I do not want to risk the exposure of letting others see me fail or allowing them to see who I really am."

8. **Feeling self-hate and self-deprecation**

   You never truly feel good about yourself. You are always cutting yourself down.

9. **Measuring your value and others' value by how well you or they perform**

   We all want to do our best and perform well. However, our self-esteem should not be measured on the basis of our performance.

10. **Rejecting or not associating with others who do not measure up**

    You avoid these people because you worry that their shortcomings might somehow reflect poorly on you and cause you shame.

Those are just some of the indicators that can let you know if you are motivated by shame. I believe every person has to deal with shame in their lives to some extent. It is a human condition. It was sin's first contribution to the human race.

The Two Goats

The second important animal to understand in reference to shame is the goat. In Leviticus, Moses writes about the important yet very distinct functions of two goats.

"Aaron shall offer the bull as a sin offering, which *is* for himself, and make atonement for himself and for his house. He shall take the two goats and present them before the Lord *at* the door of the tabernacle of meeting. Then Aaron shall cast lots for the two goats: one lot for the Lord and the other lot for the scapegoat. And Aaron shall bring the goat on which the Lord's lot fell, and offer it *as* a sin offering. But the goat on which the lot fell to be the scapegoat shall be presented alive before the Lord, to make atonement upon it, *and* to let it go as the scapegoat into the wilderness. . . . And when he has made an end of atoning for the Holy *Place*, the tabernacle of meeting, and the altar, he shall bring the live goat. Aaron shall lay both his hands on the head of the live goat, confess over it all the iniquities of the children of Israel, and all their transgressions, concerning all their sins, putting them on the head of the goat, and shall send *it* away into the wilderness by the hand of a suitable man. The goat shall bear on itself all their iniquities to an uninhabited land; and he shall release the goat in the wilderness (Leviticus 16:6–10, 20–22).

This passage is not referring to Passover, when the lamb was sacrificed. Rather, this is the Day of Atonement that happened in the fall of every year. The children of Israel annually recognized the Day of Atonement, when God provided cleansing for their sins with two goats.

God tells Aaron to take two goats and cast lots. For the one on which the Lord's lot falls, Aaron is to bring it into the tabernacle and sacrifice it for the sins of Israel. In doing so, the people's sins will be forgiven.

But there is another goat. God tells Aaron to lay his hands on the head of the second goat and pronounce over it every single sin and transgression of Israel. This scapegoat will then carry those sins and be taken by a suitable man out of the sight of the Israelites. It will go to an uninhabited place and take the people's sins far away from them.

There are two goats for atonement because there are two elements to our sin. First, sin causes a separation between God and us. One goat solves the God problem. Second, sin creates shame inside us that damages our self-image and our social and spiritual abilities. The scapegoat solves the shame problem. Praise God that He cares about us so much that He provided for our shame to be removed, not just our sins and failures erased!

God did not want shame in Israel's camp just like He did not want shame in the Garden of Eden. God cannot work—and we cannot live—in an environment of shame. He wanted the children of Israel to know that not only had He forgiven their sins, but He had forgotten their sins as well. God does not want shame to affect people's self-esteem, their relationships with each other, or their relationship with Him in any way. Therefore, He designated the second goat to be a visual symbol of shame being taken out of the camp.

When the second goat walked out of the camp, the people knew their sins were gone. In the same way, God has not only taken care of our sins, but He has taken

SIN CREATES SHAME INSIDE US THAT DAMAGES OUR SELF-IMAGE AND OUR SOCIAL AND SPIRITUAL ABILITIES.

care of our shame too. It is one thing to know we have been forgiven, but it is an entirely different thing to know that we have no shame before God.

This is our good news: *Jesus is our scapegoat.* He is not just the Lamb of God who takes away our sins. Jesus takes away our shame as well. He is the total solution for sin. In the Old Testament, a scapegoat was selected to bear the Israelites' sins every year. But Jesus is our once-for-all-time scapegoat. On the cross, He permanently removed our sin and shame. God pronounced all our sins on Jesus and sent Him "outside the camp" to bear our shame. Our sin and our shame are gone forever!

The Lamb of God

The third animal I want to talk about related to shame is the Lamb of God. Listen to this Scripture regarding John the Baptist: "John saw Jesus coming toward him, and said, 'Behold! The Lamb of God who takes away the sin of the world!'" (John 1:29). Jesus is the Lamb who takes away our sins *and* the scapegoat who takes away our shame.

Read Isaiah 53 again, remembering that the scapegoat had all the sins of Israel pronounced upon it. It was the most despised animal on the face of the earth. It had to go to an uninhabitable land, and it was rejected and despised as soon as all the sins came upon it. The language in Isaiah 53 may seem a bit different now that you know that Jesus is your scapegoat.

> He is despised and rejected by men,
> A Man of sorrows and acquainted with grief.

And we hid, as it were, *our* faces from Him;

He was despised, and we did not esteem Him.

Surely He has borne our griefs

And carried our sorrows;

Yet we esteemed Him stricken,

Smitten by God, and afflicted.

But He *was* wounded for our transgressions,

He was bruised for our iniquities;

The chastisement for our peace *was* upon Him,

And by His stripes we are healed.

All we like sheep have gone astray;

We have turned, every one, to his own way;

And the Lord has laid on Him the iniquity of us all

(Isaiah 53:3–6).

Leviticus 16:22 says, "The goat shall bear on itself all their iniquities." Isaiah 53:6 says, "The Lord has laid on Him the iniquity of us all."

When Jesus Christ died on the cross, every one of our sins were pronounced upon Him. He became our scapegoat. In the presence of the entire world, God did not just heal us of our sin issue. He healed us of our shame issue too.

There is a powerful parallel between the Garden of Eden and the cross. In the Garden of Eden, there was no shame, but there was a tree with fruit that could not be eaten. The punishment for eating the fruit was removal from the garden. When they ate the fruit, Adam and Eve sinned, lost their shamelessness, and were evicted from paradise.

GOD DID NOT JUST HEAL US OF OUR SIN ISSUE. HE HEALED US OF OUR SHAME ISSUE TOO.

On a different tree (the cross), Jesus bore our sin and shame outside the city of Jerusalem. Through His sacrifice, they have been removed forever. We have been brought back into a shameless relationship with God and each other.

Jesus Christ was a second Adam. In His nakedness and suffering, He took our shame away. Today, we can live and function totally shame-free. We can confidently confess, "Jesus died for me and took away my sin and shame. Through Jesus, I am now perfectly right with God!"

Five Steps to Overcoming Shame

Be Naked Without Shame

Of course, I am not talking about taking your clothes off. But we can be "naked"—we can be who we really are. We do not have to hide any longer.

When Jesus came into this world, He had no problems with sinners. He had problems with dishonest religious people. You will never find a story in the Bible about Jesus having a problem with someone who was honest about their sin. Jesus did take issue with people who tried to hide who they really were, though. Because Jesus has removed our shame, we can be who we really are and live in the light.

The apostle John puts it this way:

> This is the message which we have heard from Him and declare to you, that God is light and in Him is no darkness at all. If we say that we have fellowship with

Him, and walk in darkness, we lie and do not practice the truth. But if we walk in the light as He is in the light, we have fellowship with one another, and the blood of Jesus Christ His Son cleanses us from all sin.

If we say that we have no sin, we deceive ourselves, and the truth is not in us. If we confess our sins, He is faithful and just to forgive us *our* sins and to cleanse us from all unrighteousness. If we say that we have not sinned, we make Him a liar, and His word is not in us (1 John 1:5–10).

Not only have we all sinned, but we all live in a constant state of being less than we ought to be. Do you know what the good news is, then? Jesus made up the difference. Jesus, who knew no sin, became sin so we could become the righteousness of God in Christ. That means I do not have to play games. I do not have to pretend to be something I am not. God loves me in my imperfections. He just wants me to get naked and stop hiding from Him. Of course, we cannot really hide from God anyway. He could see through the fig leaves that Adam and Eve tried to use to hide their nakedness, and He can see through us as well.

In his letter John tells believers that God exists in the light, and in Him there is no darkness whatsoever. When we walk honestly and openly, we have good relationships with God and other people. However, we only deceive ourselves if we claim to be perfect. I may measure up to other people, but I can never measure up to God. And He is fine with that.

In 2 Corinthians 12:8–10 the apostle Paul says,

Concerning this thing I pleaded with the Lord three times that it might depart from me. And He said to me, "My grace is sufficient for you, for My strength is made perfect in weakness." Therefore most gladly I will rather boast in my infirmities, that the power of Christ may rest upon me. Therefore I take pleasure in infirmities, in reproaches, in needs, in persecutions, in distresses, for Christ's sake. For when I am weak, then I am strong.

We don't know what Paul's "thorn" was. Based on his comments in the book of Colossians, some say it may have been a vision problem. Whatever it was, it kept Paul from being the person he wanted to be, so he went to God and said, "Please take this thing away."

Paul had been an elite Pharisee; he was raised to be a perfect religious person, always performing and always pretending to be faultless. God said, *Sorry, Paul. You are just going to have to depend on My grace, for My power is made perfect in your weakness. In your vulnerabilities and what you cannot do or accomplish alone, that is where I am going to perfect My power.*

We all sin, and we all fall short of God's glory (Romans 3:23). Our tendency is to try to cover up our problems and act like nothing is wrong. God sees through us, though. No matter how imperfect you are, you can jump onto His lap at the throne of grace, and He will love and enjoy you anyway. You do not have to play games with God. He is a real God, and He is okay with us.

Satan wants to put shame on us because when we are living in shame, we cannot go to God. Shame says, "Get your act together, and then you can talk to God." The problem is that we cannot get our act together *until* we talk to God.

There is no power in shame. There is no grace in shame. There is no freedom in shame. Shame is a prison that keeps us in the bondage of our sins. We can only be set free when we understand that not only are we forgiven, but our shame is gone too.

God removes shame from our lives, and He is okay with us. There is no reproach. There is no reason to fear. Remember, Adam and Eve hid because they were afraid of God. You do not have to fear God. He loves you just the way you are right now.

Take Responsibility for Your Own Behavior

We must take responsibility for our behavior and stop blaming other people.

When Adam and Eve hid themselves, God walked up to them and said, *Adam, what have you done?* Here is what Adam said: *Eve made me do it.* Men still use that excuse all the time today—"It is that woman You gave me. She is my problem." Then God went to Eve and said, *Eve, what have you done*? She replied, *The devil made me do it.*

This Scripture demonstrates an important principle because they were both telling the truth. Eve was the one who talked to the devil first, and she was the one who ate first and then gave the fruit to Adam. But Adam was a grown man; he did not have to eat it. Even though Eve did all those things, it was not her fault that Adam ate the fruit. His eating was his own fault. Adam turned and confessed his sins over Eve and tried to make her bear them, but God did not accept Eve as Adam's scapegoat.

Eve also told the truth—the devil did tempt her. The devil was party to her eating that fruit. The problem is that, like Adam, she was still responsible for her own actions. Eve turned and laid her hands on the devil and tried to make him bear her sins, but God didn't accept the devil as Eve's scapegoat either. Instead, He cursed Adam, Eve, and the serpent and kicked them out of the garden.

Now here is my personal opinion about this situation: if Adam and Eve would have owned their behavior and not blamed somebody else, I do not believe that God would have kicked them out of the Garden of Eden. That is just my personal opinion; it may not be true. But they were cursed and kicked out, and I believe it was because they found their own scapegoats and would not take responsibility for their actions.

There is a difference between confession and repentance. *Confession* means telling the truth about my sins and problems. *Repentance* means taking responsibility for my behavior and making wrong things right. If we will take responsibility for our behavior, Jesus will bear our shame as our scapegoat. If we won't, then we will find our own scapegoat, and we will not be set free.

Parents are often chosen to fill the scapegoat role. People say, "I know I am messed up, but you should have seen my parents. They did this to me!" There is no particular requirement for someone to be chosen

IF WE WILL TAKE
RESPONSIBILITY FOR
OUR BEHAVIOR, JESUS
WILL BEAR OUR SHAME
AS OUR SCAPEGOAT.

as a scapegoat. It might be your sibling, friend, or coworker. Maybe it is a leader at your church or a government official. Someone else—anyone else—can be your scapegoat. The problem is that having any other scapegoat besides Jesus will not work.

You lay hands on your spouse; you lay hands on your parents; you lay hands on the government. You confess your sins over them and think that someone will accept that. But God does not accept it. My sin is not anyone else's problem. My sin is my problem, and God will help me if I will take responsibility for what I am doing right now. The only scapegoat that God recognizes is Jesus Christ, the Righteous One. He is the *only* one. He will not bear our sins until we take responsibility and get honest about our behavior.

Second Corinthians 7:10 says, "Godly sorrow produces repentance *leading* to salvation, not to be regretted." Lack of shame does not mean lack of personal responsibility and effort to do my best. It simply means that my best is still lacking, but God is not ashamed of me, and I do not have to be ashamed of myself either. I can fail without being a failure.

Jesus died on the cross to remove our sin and shame, not to produce a bunch of sanctified cowards or eternal victims. He died so we could be overcomers like Him!

Believe You Are Forgiven and Shame Has Been Removed

How do you know that you are forgiven of your sins? You just have to put your faith in Jesus. First John 1:9 says,

"If we confess our sins, He is faithful and just to forgive us *our* sins and to cleanse us from all unrighteousness."

The English word *confess* is the Greek word *homolagao*. *Homo* means "same," and *lagao* means "word"—"same word." If we will say what God is saying about our behavior—if we will just tell the truth—He will take away our sins.

Here is how David put it:

> The Lord *is* merciful and gracious,
> Slow to anger, and abounding in mercy.
> He will not always strive *with us,*
> Nor will He keep *His anger* forever.
> He has not dealt with us according to our sins,
> Nor punished us according to our iniquities.
> For as the heavens are high above the earth,
> *So* great is His mercy toward those who fear Him;
> As far as the east is from the west,
> *So* far has He removed our transgressions from us.
> As a father pities *his children,*
> *So* the Lord pities those who fear Him.
> For He knows our frame;
> He remembers that we *are* dust (Psalm 103:8–14).

Isn't that a wonderful passage? "As far as the east is from the west." God has an ability that we do not: the ability to forget. As people, we remember things. When someone does something to us, we can forgive that person, but we still remember. God can forget. As far as the east is from the west, He removes our sin. The shame is completely gone.

When we come to God, confess our sins, and take responsibility for our behavior, we say, "Lord, I pray that You would forgive me." God replies, "I do forgive you! By the blood of My Son you are forgiven. And not only are you forgiven, but I put it away as far as the east is from the west."

God forgets those sins; they are gone for all eternity. His behavior toward you is just like a person who completely forgot what you did. You are favored, and you are loved; you do not have to carry the shame.

The opposite is someone who never forgets and never lets you forget either. Every time you do something wrong, they say, "Remember?" That is what the devil says to us. "Remember your moral failure? Remember your abortion? Remember when you stole that thing? Remember your divorce? Remember what you did? Remember what you said?" He wants you to go back and constantly relive all the problems of your past. That is not the spirit of God. When God forgives sin, it is forgotten. He never brings it up a second time, and He never remembers it again for all eternity.

Fight Satan with the Blood and the Word

When Satan attacks you with a spirit of shame and condemnation, fight him with the blood of Jesus and the Word of God.

The devil will attack you. Every time you do something wrong, he will try to bring condemnation and shame so that he can keep you away from God. He wants to make

WHEN GOD FORGIVES SIN, IT IS FORGOTTEN.

you feel like a failure and keep you from relating to other people in the right way.

Romans 8:1 says, *"There is* therefore now no condemnation to those who are in Christ Jesus, who do not walk according to the flesh, but according to the Spirit." There is *no* condemnation. You fight the devil with the word *kataphronesas*. Scripture says that Jesus despised the shame—He mentally battled against it. We have to learn to take the Word of God and fight Satan with it.

Listen to what Johns writes in Revelation.

> Then I heard a loud voice saying in heaven, "Now salvation, and strength, and the kingdom of our God, and the power of His Christ have come, for the accuser of our brethren, who accused them before our God day and night, has been cast down. And they overcame him by the blood of the Lamb and by the word of their testimony, and they did not love their lives to the death (Revelation 12:10–11).

How do we overcome Satan? *By the blood of the Lamb and the word of our testimony.* Someone told me something many years ago, and it works every time. When Satan begins to talk to you about your sin and tries to put shame and condemnation on you, just begin to praise Jesus for His blood. It will stop the enemy every time. Satan hates the name of Jesus and hates any mention of the blood of Jesus. The blood of Jesus is what cancels out our sins and defeats Satan. Demonic spirits cannot stand in the presence of praise and worship or the mention of Jesus and His blood. When you are being attacked with thoughts or feelings of shame and condemnation, just raise up your voice by faith and begin to quote the Word of God. Thank Jesus for His blood and what He has done for you. It will defeat Satan every single time.

You have to fight the demonic spirit of shame. You have to war against it. You cannot let it get into your head. If it is already in your head, you have to take those thoughts captive and reject them from your mind. Shame is a stronghold that will keep you in bondage until you take it captive and cast it out by the authority of God and His Word—just like Jesus did.

Forgive Every Person Who Has Shamed or Hurt You

The final step is to forgive every person who has hurt you or helped to produce shame in your life. You may have been abused, raped, had something done to you, or been publicly embarrassed. Someone may have used shame to try to control you or to control your behavior.

It could have been your parents. It could have been a church. It could have been somebody else. Please listen carefully: God will never minister more grace to us than we are willing to give away to other people. If we want mercy and grace in our lives, we have to give it away—to our parents, our siblings, our friends, and every other person who has helped to produce shame or hurt in our lives.

HOW DO WE OVERCOME
SATAN? BY THE BLOOD
OF THE LAMB AND
THE WORD OF OUR
TESTIMONY.

We were created to live without shame. A serpent ruined that in the Garden of Eden, but a goat and a lamb solved that problem on the cross. Now we can live free from the curse of shame for all eternity.

5

OVERCOMING
UNFORGIVENESS

WE ALL WILL experience offenses, hurts, unkind words, rejection, and betrayal at some point in our lives. These painful interactions will often involve close friends or family members but can also come from strangers or acquaintances. Regardless of the source, we must forgive.

Matthew 18 contains a very poignant story about the necessity of forgiveness.

> Then Peter came to Him [Jesus] and said, "Lord, how often shall my brother sin against me, and I forgive him? Up to seven times?"
>
> Jesus said to him, "I do not say to you, up to seven times, but up to seventy times seven. Therefore the kingdom of heaven is like a certain king who wanted to settle accounts with his servants. And when he had begun to settle accounts, one was brought to him who owed him ten thousand talents. But as he was not able to pay, his master commanded that he be sold, with his wife and children and all that he had, and that payment be made. The servant therefore fell down before him, saying, 'Master, have patience with me, and

I will pay you all.' Then the master of that servant was moved with compassion, released him, and forgave him the debt.

But that servant went out and found one of his fellow servants who owed him a hundred denarii; and he laid hands on him and took *him* by the throat, saying, 'Pay me what you owe!' So his fellow servant fell down at his feet and begged him, saying, 'Have patience with me, and I will pay you all.' And he would not, but went and threw him into prison till he should pay the debt. So when his fellow servants saw what had been done, they were very grieved, and came and told their master all that had been done. Then his master, after he had called him, said to him, 'You wicked servant! I forgave you all that debt because you begged me. Should you not also have had compassion on your fellow servant, just as I had pity on you?' And his master was angry, and delivered him to the torturers until he should pay all that was due to him.

So My heavenly Father also will do to you if each of you, from his heart, does not forgive his brother his trespasses" (Matthew 18:21–35).

This is a shocking story, but Jesus has a specific purpose for telling it. He uses this hyperbole to illustrate three shocking truths about how God sees the issue of unforgiveness.

Three Shocking Truths Concerning Unforgiveness

It Is Shocking How Seriously God Takes the Issue of Unforgiveness

In the story, the forgiven man refuses to extend forgiveness to his fellow servant. Because of his hard heart, the forgiveness of his own debt is revoked, and he is turned over to torturers. Jesus says the same thing will be done to those who do not forgive others. *Torture* is a pretty strong word. Truthfully, though, unforgiveness is torture. It is a torturous lifestyle in every way.

Many physical problems can be traced back to unforgiveness in a person's life. These problems include ulcers, nerve issues, heart issues, headaches, skin irritants, and high blood pressure. Unforgiveness is also emotional torture. It wreaks havoc on our bodies and our minds. Outbursts of anger, mood swings, increased stress, personality changes, depression, anxiety, and cynicism can all be linked to unforgiveness.

Depression is an epidemic in America. The number one clinical definition of depression is *anger turned inward*. Internal anger is the highest consumer of our emotional energy, of which we all have a very limited amount. Even after positive or exciting life events—such as winning the lottery, receiving a raise, having a baby, or winning an Olympic gold medal—many people experience some depression. Why? Our emotions have to catch up. We are very limited in what we can do emotionally, so any time we expend a high level of emotional energy, it takes time for us to recharge.

It took years for me to understand that a preacher's worst day is always Monday. When I started preaching, I would always feel down when I woke up on Mondays. Years later, I still am flat on that day. It is because I spend all my emotional energy on Saturdays and Sundays. I have learned that it takes about 24 hours or so for my emotions to catch back up, and that is when something good is happening.

Human beings were not created to be repositories for anger. We just were not designed that way. If anger is the biggest consumer of emotional energy, imagine what happens after just a day or two of feeling nonstop anger and unforgiveness. Your emotions begin to crater, and you get depressed. You may not be able to hear them, but your emotions are saying, "We cannot keep up! We cannot do this. We were not designed to hate." When we cling to anger and unforgiveness, we are insuring major emotional problems in our lives.

Unforgiveness is also spiritual torture. Not only do we separate ourselves from God's grace and peace, but I also strongly believe that unforgiveness exposes us to demonic torment. Ephesians 4:26–27 says, "'Be angry, and do not sin': do not let the sun go down on your wrath, nor give place to the devil." The word "devil" in this passage comes from *diabolos*, which means "slander."

There is nothing wrong with anger. We all get angry, and it is inevitable that you will get angry at times in

IF YOU REFUSE TO FORGIVE, YOU WALK OUT FROM UNDER GOD'S WINGS AND ONTO SATAN'S PROPERTY.

your life. The problem is when we do not deal with our anger. When you "let the sun go down on your wrath," you give an opening to *diabolos*—the devil.

The devil actively looks for ways to come into our lives and cause division of every kind. He will slander your spouse, friends, coworkers, and all the other people in your life until he has divided all of your relationships. The devil causes social divisions too, such as racism, violence, lawsuits, and even wars. This is the demonic torment we open ourselves up to when we do not deal with our anger correctly.

As a child, I spent my summers on my grandfather's farm where he kept 500 chickens. Twice a day I had to gather eggs from 500 chickens. I know chickens, and I can tell you that I quickly learned to leave a hen with her chicks alone. Hens are the most protective animals; they are more dangerous than a bear! When those little chicks run under their mother's wings, the hen is ready for war. She will peck your face off!

In Matthew 23:37 Jesus mourns for Jerusalem and says, "How often I wanted to gather your children together, as a hen gathers her chicks under *her* wings, but you were not willing!" Love and forgiveness are God's property. When you are walking in forgiveness, you are walking under His covering. Hate, on the other hand, is the devil's territory. If you refuse to forgive, you walk out from under God's wings and onto Satan's property. You expose yourself to torture and torment.

Three Key Points Concerning Forgiveness

1. **The poison of unforgiveness damages the vessel it is stored in worse than anything you can spit it on.**
   In other words, unforgiveness harms *you* much more than the people with whom you are angry.

2. **Forgiveness does not make others right; it just makes us free.**
   I am not saying that what someone else did is alright. I am not saying that it can be excused. I am just saying that I want to be free, and I do not want to walk with this in my heart.

3. **Forgiveness is one of the most self-loving things you will ever do.**
   The issue of forgiveness is more about you than anyone else. If you love yourself, forgive.

Matthew 6:15 says, "If you do not forgive men their trespasses, neither will your Father forgive your trespasses." God will not forgive our sins if we do not forgive others. If you are a Christian, and there is a person in your life whom you have not forgiven in a year, all your sins for the last year have not been forgiven. It does not matter whether you have confessed them or not.

That is the shocking truth of this story. God will only give us as much grace as we will give away. If we will not forgive others, He will not forgive us.

It Is Shocking How Petty Unforgiveness
Seems from God's Perspective

Jesus' story of unforgiveness in Matthew 18 must have seemed especially ridiculous to His disciples because of the sums of money involved. The first servant owed his master "ten thousand talents" (v. 24). A talent was a massive amount of money—approximately 60–70 pounds of gold. One estimate places the talent's worth as high as $300,000. At that rate, ten thousand talents would equal three billion dollars. Jesus is speaking of a bizarre amount of money that nobody could ever pay back.

This man owed his master a three-billion-dollar debt. His only option was to beg for mercy, knowing that he, his wife, and his children would otherwise be sold to repay the unpayable debt. This man would have to work 200,000 years to pay off his debt. Incredibly, the master forgives him, and he is now debt-free. It is a miracle!

Then this debt-free man finds one of his fellow servants who owes him 100 denarii. That was equivalent to about three month's wages for a soldier or laborer at that time and probably worth about $10,000.

You would think that a person who has been released from billions of dollars of debt would be in a forgiving mood. So it is very surprising when he grabs the other servant by the throat and demands, "Pay me what you owe!" (v. 28). The servant does not have the money, so he asks for patience and promises to pay when he can. Instead of extending the same forgiveness he was shown, though, the debt-free man throws the servant into prison until the debt is repaid.

We live in a world full of hurting people, problems, and wars. We see racism, bigotry, sexism, and all forms of hatred. But Jesus says the kingdom of heaven is not like that. He draws the curtain open and says, *Let Me show you what the kingdom of heaven is like.* We have a very forgiving King, and He is willing to forgive us for all of our sins—more than we could ever repay. We simply have to be willing to forgive other people. In comparison to what we have done to Jesus, others have done very little to us. It is ridiculous for us to withhold forgiveness in light of God's incredible grace toward us.

It Is Shocking How Different We Are from God Regarding Forgiveness

Peter comes to Jesus and says, "Lord, how often shall my brother sin against me, and I forgive him? Up to seven times?" (Matthew 18:21). Here is what Jesus did *not* say: *No, Peter, eight.* He didn't say, *No, Peter, 12 . . . or 40—those are more biblical numbers. That is a lot, Peter, but you can get there.* Jesus says, "Up to seventy times seven" (v. 22). The point is that you *always* forgive.

> The Lord *is* merciful and gracious,
> Slow to anger, and abounding in mercy.
> He will not always strive *with us,*
> Nor will He keep *His anger* forever.
> He has not dealt with us according to our sins,
> Nor punished us according to our iniquities.
> For as the heavens are high above the earth,

IN COMPARISON TO
WHAT WE HAVE DONE
TO JESUS, OTHERS HAVE
DONE VERY LITTLE TO US.

So great is His mercy toward those who fear Him;
As far as the east is from the west,
So far has He removed our transgressions from us.
As a father pities *his* children,
So the Lord pities those who fear Him.
For He knows our frame;
He remembers that we *are* dust (Psalm 103:8–14).

Our God is so incredibly forgiving. That is why I love Him. Of course, there are many reasons to love Jesus, but He is the nicest, most gracious, and most merciful person I have ever met. He has had countless reasons to ditch me, but there is no one as loving or as merciful as God. He is so much different than we are in that area.

According to a nationwide poll, 94 percent of Americans believe it is important to forgive, but only half of Americans make it a regular practice. There are many believers today who walk in unforgiveness and feel completely justified. But they are not! We must learn to be forgiving people.

Understanding the Meaning of Forgiveness

If we are going to become forgiving people, we need to understand the true meaning of forgiveness. Based on Jesus' parable of the unforgiving servant, here are three concepts of what forgiveness is.

Permanently Forgiving All Debt and Bringing the Balance to Zero

In Jesus' story, the master forgives his servant's enormous debt. He does not make him pay most of it, some of it, or even a little bit of it. He forgives the entire debt and absorbs the cost himself. However, the servant is not willing to do the same for his fellow man. The master rebukes him, saying "You wicked servant! I forgave you all that debt because you begged me. Should you not also have had compassion on your fellow servant, just as I had pity on you?" (Matthew 18:32–33).

The Greek word for forgive is *aphiemi* and means "to leave" or "to send away." Forgiveness says, "I completely and permanently release the offense I have against you. It does not matter if I have been damaged, hurt, offended, or embarrassed. I do not require an apology or an explanation. You do not have to pay me back. I will absorb the cost. I will pay the price. The balance between us is zero."

How do you know if you have forgiven someone? One way is to see if that same issue keeps coming up. If it does, you have not forgiven them. Also, there is no such thing as conditional forgiveness—"I forgive you, but if you do that again ..." If it's conditional, it's not forgiveness.

Permanently Forfeiting the Right of Reproach

Forgiveness says, "I will not try to harm you for this. I will not talk badly about you. I will not try to hurt you physically. I will not try to pay you back somehow or get

THERE IS NO SUCH THING AS CONDITIONAL FORGIVENESS.

you to pay for what you have done. I will not reproach you about this."

Permanently Forgoing All Expressions of Private and Public Judgment

Forgiveness says, "I will not judge this issue any longer. I will not talk badly about you privately or publicly. I will not try to hurt you by the things I say about you."

When you forgive someone, you release all judgment of them to God. You refuse to engage in name-calling and finger-pointing. You trust God to be a fair judge, and as far as you are concerned, the debt is paid in full.

What Forgiveness Does Not Mean

Whenever I teach on this subject, there are always people who come to me and say, "But Jimmy, what about this or that situation?" I hope to cover any concerns you may have by telling you what forgiveness does *not* mean.

Forgiveness Does Not Mean I Lose the Right of Self-Protection

Jesus says, "Be wise as serpents and harmless as doves" (Matthew 10:16). Forgiving someone does not mean I have to be best friends with that person or return to a potentially abusive or dangerous situation. You can forgive and still protect yourself. You do not have to let yourself be a target for further abuse. There are people I

FORGIVENESS SIMPLY MEANS THAT YOU GIVE UP THE RIGHT TO DECIDE THE PUNISHMENT.

have forgiven who are not safe or compatible with me, so I choose not to be around them.

Forgiveness Does Not Mean I Have No Basis for Confrontation

I can forgive someone but still confront them. In Ephesians 4:15 the apostle Paul tells believers to speak "the truth in love." I may forgive Karen for something she has done, or she may forgive me for something I have done, but we still need to sit down and talk about it. This applies especially to the people with whom you are the closest. Confrontation, when done correctly, is an important step to rebuilding relationships and gaining understanding.

Remember, though, that forgiveness is not based on the confrontation's outcome. Even if the other person does not respond well to what you have to say, you choose to forgive them anyway. Forgiveness is not conditional on agreement.

Forgiveness Does Not Mean There Should Not Be Punishment or Consequences

We have all heard of heart-wrenching situations in which someone is murdered, and the victim's family forgives the individual who committed the crime. That does not mean, however, that the murderer does not need to go to jail. In some circumstances, there must be consequences for words and actions. Forgiveness simply means that you give up the right to decide the punishment. You choose not to seek *vengeance*.

Forgiveness Does Not Mean I Cannot Seek
Legal or Police Protection

I can forgive someone for something they did that was illegal, but I may still need to call the police or seek legal protection. Forgiveness does not mean we have to put ourselves in harm's way.

Here is the main question regarding forgiveness: *what is my motive in all of these issues?* If your honest response is God's glory and the good of everyone involved, then your heart is right. However, if your motive is revenge or vindication, then it is likely based in unforgiveness. Unforgiveness can take many forms, including

- revenge (murder, violence, abuse)
- hate
- verbal abuse (slander, gossip, sarcasm, labeling, name-calling)
- divorce
- rejection and avoidance for punishment's sake
- withholding good
- transference of affection
- prejudice, bigotry, racism, or sexism
- bitterness
- internally wishing for bad things to happen to someone
- praying against someone

The bottom line is we must deal honestly and thoroughly with this issue. Otherwise, we will suffer serious consequences.

How to Forgive from the Heart

In His parable, Jesus says that if you do not forgive your brother from your *heart*, God will turn you over to tormenters. What we have been talking about so far are the technical issues of forgiveness. However, Jesus makes clear that forgiveness is primarily a heart issue.

Our Sins Cost Jesus His Life

The first key to forgiving from the heart is remembering that our sins cost Jesus His life. The unforgiving servant forgot his master's sacrifice, and we often do the exact same thing. The most righteous person in the history of the world died the worst death in the history of the world, and you and I put Him there. The Jews did not put Him there. The Romans did not put Him there. Our sins—yours and mine—put Him there.

One of the bad things about unforgiveness is that much of the time, we actually feel good about it. We feel justified in our bitterness and bad behavior. We point to what a person has done and declare, "You just don't understand what they did! I would *never* do that!"

You may be accurate in that you would never repeat a certain wrongdoing, but we have *all* done bad things. Do we understand what we did to Jesus and what He had to endure because of us? Our sins put Jesus on that cross.

FORGIVENESS IS PRIMARILY A HEART ISSUE.

Our wrongdoings hammered the nails, thrust the spear, cracked the whip, put on the crown of thorns, and nailed up the sign mocking Him as the King of the Jews.

Someone may owe you the emotional equivalent of 100 denarii, but for what you did to Jesus, you owe Him billions of dollars. Make that trillions while you are at it. You could never begin to repay even the interest on what you owe Jesus. But He forgave you, and He forgave me. That is our great truth. Once we understand it, we will have a different attitude about everything, including forgiveness.

We cannot extend forgiveness to others if our own hearts are hardened with pride. We must begin by simply admitting, "I may not have done that particular wrong thing, but I did enough wrong to put Jesus on the cross. I owe Him everything."

God Loves Our Offenders as Much as He Loves Us

The second key to forgiving from the heart is to remember that God loves our offenders as much as He loves us. This is the offensive part for many people. When someone has done something horrible to us, we feel justified because we feel that we are better than they are.

All unforgiveness begins with labeling and de-valuing. We think that by putting a label on someone, we have the right to withhold forgiveness and mistreat that person. However, all humans beings are sacred in God's sight, and He loves them more than we can comprehend. The unforgiving servant thought he was special and more deserving of forgiveness than the other man, but he was absolutely wrong. John 3:16 does not say that Jesus came to save only a select few. No, He came so that *"whoever* believes in Him should not perish but have everlasting life" (emphasis mine).

Perhaps as you are reading this chapter, you are thinking of some people you need to forgive. Some people are frustrating, but we find it fairly easy to forgive them and believe God still loves them. Others are a bit more challenging to forgive because they are difficult or hurtful, but we somehow find a way to release those offenses as well.

But then there are the devastators. Every person has a devastator in his or her life, and this is the hardest person to think about forgiving. This person did something, said something, or failed to do or say something, and it absolutely devastated you. Your experience was so painful that you cannot imagine God feeling the same way about them that He does about you.

I understand this statement may feel really offensive, but it is the truth: God loves the person who devastated you as much as He loves you. He really does. Think of any terrorist, mass murderer, or evil dictator who has ever existed. That person was formed in their mother's womb by God. We see such people as evil and believe our hatred of them is justified, but do you know how God sees them? He sees them as children on their way to hell. God does not overlook or excuse their behavior by any means, but He simply does not hate them the way we do.

GOD LOVES THE PERSON
WHO DEVASTATED
YOU AS MUCH AS HE
LOVES YOU.

As I said before, we put labels on people in an attempt to justify our hate. We may think that because we are born-again, Spirit-filled Christians, God loves us more than He loves anybody else. We could not be more wrong, though. Look at John 3:16 again: "For God so loved the world ..." *World*. It does not say "America." It does not even say "Christians." When Jesus says *world*, He means every single person who has ever lived or ever will live. We have no right to hate any person Jesus died to save, and He died to save us all.

Do you realize that most of the New Testament was written by a man who once killed Christians for a living? Before he met Jesus on the road to Damascus and became an apostle, missionary, and evangelist, Paul purposefully and strategically targeted Christians. Acts 7:58 records his presence at the murder of Stephen, the first Christian martyr. Believers in the early church feared and hated Paul, but Jesus loved him enough to appear to him in person and change the entire trajectory of his life.

Regardless of what people have done to us, they're still human beings in God's sight. They are still His most precious creation. Until they draw their very last breath, God will chase them to the gates of hell to try to get them to heaven.

We Permanently Release Debt and Judgment

The third key to forgiving from your heart is making a permanent release of others' debts and judgments to

God. A better way to say this is that we have to disqualify ourselves as judges.

We do not make good judges of people, and the main reason is because we usually only see their *behavior*. We all see people's actions, but rarely do we know *why* they do what they do. As a pastor, I hear stories about the devastation in people's lives all the time. Devastation will change a person. You may see a person from the outside, and all you can focus on is their idiosyncrasies and quirks. We all tend to judge other people until we hear their stories.

Only God knows everybody's story. Therefore, He is the only one qualified to judge. To forgive from my heart, I put Jesus there. He loves everybody as much as He loves me, and I am not qualified to judge anyone. The apostle Paul understands this when he writes,

> Repay no one evil for evil. Have regard for good things in the sight of all men. If it is possible, as much as depends on you, live peaceably with all men. Beloved, do not avenge yourselves, but *rather* give place to wrath; for it is written, "Vengeance is *Mine*, I will repay," says the Lord (Romans 12:17–19).

Unforgiveness is unbelief. It says, "I don't trust God to handle this situation for me." Forgiveness says, "I release this person, and if any judgment is needed, I trust God to take care of it." We must put judgment into God's hands. He is qualified, and we are not.

ONLY GOD KNOWS
EVERYBODY'S STORY.
THEREFORE, HE IS THE
ONLY ONE QUALIFIED
TO JUDGE.

We Bless and Pray for Our Enemies

The fourth key to forgiving from your heart—and this is a big one—is we must bless our enemies and pray for them. In Luke 6:28 Jesus says, "Bless those who curse you, and pray for those who spitefully use you."

I want to go back to the word *devastate*. Yes, people who are frustrating, difficult, and hurtful can be challenging, but the devastators are the real issue. So many times I hear people say, "Jimmy, I want to forgive, and I keep saying every day that I forgive them. The hate is still there, though, and I feel bad about it. What do I do?"

I understand that. I do not believe I am a hateful person, but there have been two or three people in my life whom I have hated. You have to work hard to get me to hate you, and they did. I *hated* them. My hatred was oppressive and tormenting; it was the torture I talked about earlier in this chapter.

The healing of my emotions only came as I prayed for those people. Now, I certainly did *not* want to pray for them, and I was very offended when God told me to do so. Many times I felt like saying, "Lord, I do not want You to bless them. I can pray anything good, but I do not mean it. I want You to hurt them." But Jesus commands us to pray for our enemies and bless them.

If you cannot pray for someone, then you have not forgiven them. Blessings force forgiveness from our heads to our hearts. You do not have to go through some ritualistic type of performance or pretense where you just speak the words and walk away carrying all your ill will. God says, *Forgive from your heart, or it is not going to work with Me.* Why? Because He is a heart-God.

The person who devastated you may be alive, or they may be dead. It does not matter. You just keep blessing them until you get healed. When you start giving grace away, God will start giving grace into your heart. As you pray for them, you will be healed. That is how I changed. That is how I stopped hated those people. I prayed for them, and love and forgiveness replaced the hate in my heart.

We Resist Satan

The fifth and final key to forgiving from your heart is that you have to resist Satan. He will always come and try to stir up old issues and reoffend you. He also tries to get us to pick up everybody else's offenses, as if we do not have enough of our own.

Revelation 12:10 calls Satan " the accuser of the brethren," and we must learn to recognize his accusations against our spouses, friends, coworkers, authority figures, etc. Remember, forgiveness is spiritual warfare. Here are some action points to help you resist Satan's attacks.

- Don't go to bed angry.
- Deal with offenses and hurts every day.
- Don't take up other people's offenses.
- Don't rehearse and nurse hurts.

REMEMBER, FORGIVENESS IS SPIRITUAL WARFARE.

- Reverse hurts by forgiving, blessing, and loving your enemies.
- Don't justify unforgiveness, self-pity, or bitterness.

———————

Satan wants to keep us separated from God and each other. Decide right now that you are going to overcome unforgiveness. Begin by recognizing that you have been forgiven a huge debt that you could never repay and then release any judgments you have to the Lord. Allow Jesus to begin the work of showing His amazing love for others through you.

6

OVERCOMING DISCOURAGEMENT

IN ADDITION TO shame and fear, I believe the devil has another powerful weapon that he frequently uses against us: *discouragement.* The enemy will do everything in his power to keep us from fulfilling God's plan for our lives. He wants us to be so overwhelmed by our circumstances that we just give up and stop doing what God has called us to do.

David was a fearless shepherd, a valiant warrior, and a champion of the faith. However, he also had some incredibly low points when all the odds seemed to be against him. In one of the worst times of his life, David fought against discouragement by encouraging himself in the Lord. The book of 1 Samuel records this example of encouragement.

> Now it happened, when David and his men came to Ziklag, on the third day, that the Amalekites had invaded the South and Ziklag, attacked Ziklag and burned it with fire, and had taken captive the women and those who *were* there, from small to great; they did not kill anyone, but carried *them* away and went their way. So David and his men came to the city, and there it was, burned with

fire; and their wives, their sons, and their daughters had been taken captive. Then David and the people who *were* with him lifted up their voices and wept, until they had no more power to weep. And David's two wives, Ahinoam the Jezreelitess, and Abigail the widow of Nabal the Carmelite, had been taken captive. Now David was greatly distressed, for the people spoke of stoning him, because the soul of all the people was grieved, every man for his sons and his daughters. **But David strengthened himself in the Lord his God.**

Then David said to Abiathar the priest, Ahimelech's son, "Please bring the ephod here to me." And Abiathar brought the ephod to David. So David inquired of the Lord, saying, "Shall I pursue this troop? Shall I overtake them?"

And He answered him, "Pursue, for you shall surely overtake *them* and without fail recover *all*" (1 Samuel 30:1–8, emphasis mine).

David's background story begins in 1 Samuel 16. His father, Jesse, is a Jewish man who lives in the town of Bethlehem and has eight sons. David is the youngest son, and he takes care of his father's flocks of sheep. One day, the prophet Samuel arrives and invites Jesse and his sons to join him in a ritual sacrifice. They do not know that the prophet is actually there because God has sent him to anoint one of Jesse's sons as the new king of Israel. King Saul is currently the ruler, but he has disobeyed God repeatedly. Samuel has warned Saul that his disobedience has caused God to reject him as king, but Saul does not realize that Samuel is actually going to anoint a new king of God's choosing.

Jesse presents his seven older sons to Samuel while David stays behind with the sheep. The prophet is initially impressed with the older brothers, but God is not. He tells Samuel, *"The Lord does* not *see* as man sees; for man looks at the outward appearance, but the Lord looks at the heart" (v. 7). Samuel asks to see the youngest son, and when David arrives, God immediately tells the prophet, "Arise, anoint him; for this *is* the one!" (v. 12). Samuel anoints David in front of the older brothers, and "the Spirit of the Lord came upon David from that day forward" (v. 13).

You might think that being selected by God to be the next king would ensure an easy and happy life for David. However, from the moment Samuel anoints the young man, almost everything in David's life becomes much more difficult.

Yes, David does kill the Philistine giant Goliath, and his success wins the attention and admiration of the people of Israel. However, King Saul becomes extremely jealous. The ruler tries to kill David by throwing spears at him, and David has to flee for his life. King Saul pursues David all around Israel, and finally David has to leave the country and take refuge with the Philistines.

In 1 Samuel 29 David gets kicked out of the Philistine camp. Saul still wants to kill him, and the enemy no longer wants anything to do with him. David and his men return to Ziklag and find that the Amalekites have invaded the city, taken their families captive, and set the place on fire.

David's men are the most courageous men in the world, and they are intensely loyal to David. They have followed him from the comfort of their homes to enemy territory and back again. But seeing their burned city and fearing for the lives of their loved ones greatly discourages them. They all cry until they cannot cry anymore, and then they start talking about stoning David.

If you ever wanted to know what a bad day looks like, read that story one more time. David was having a *bad* day. But even in the middle of all the chaos, confusion, and distress , he encouraged himself in the Lord. This demonstrates an important truth: discouragement is not a condition; it is a choice.

All of us get discouraged. You may be mildly discouraged right now about something, or you may be really discouraged about something else. You may be overwhelmed or even depressed. As long as we live on this earth, the devil will attack us with discouragement from time to time.

Though any of us can become discouraged, staying there is a choice. When David heard about his wives and children being taken captive, he obviously got discouraged. He sat down and cried as hard as he possibly could, but then he made a choice—he was not going to stay there. David refused to let the grief of that moment overwhelm him. Instead, he stood up and encouraged himself in the Lord.

DISCOURAGEMENT IS NOT A CONDITION; IT IS A CHOICE.

Three Keys to Overcoming Discouragement

Even in the worst of times, we can overcome discouragement as we learn to encourage ourselves in the Lord. Here are three keys to overcoming discouragement.

A Godward Mindset

Having a Godward mindset means focusing your mind toward God. David was a master at this skill.

The book of Psalms has 150 individuals songs, and 73 of those are attributed to David. This man was a worshipper. He wrote many of his songs during very difficult times in his life, which is why they are so comforting and encouraging to us today. Nothing ministers to my heart more than the book of Psalms, especially when I am going through a tough time.

David's songs share his secret of staying encouraged even in troubling times.

> I have set the LORD always before me
> Because *He is* at my right hand I shall not be moved
> (Psalm 16:8).

That is a *Godward* mindset. The devil, on the other hand, wants you to have is a *godless* mindset. He wants you to see the giants, the mountains, and the problems, but he does not want you to see God.

David chose to see God in everything. That is why he did not get overwhelmed in bad times. When the Philistine giant Goliath taunted the Israelite army, all the trained soldiers literally shook in their boots from fear. Then David showed up. He was only a boy with a slingshot, but he looked directly at the giant and said, "You come to me with a sword, with a spear, and with a javelin. But I come to you in the name of the Lord of hosts, the God of the armies of Israel" (1 Samuel 17:45). David saw God in everything.

That is a choice we can all make. God is always right there with us. However, our attitude and state of mind have everything to do with our choice to acknowledge God or not. If we do not see Him in our circumstances, we will find ourselves absolutely overwhelmed.

Let's look at Psalm 59. Its introduction tells the exact circumstances surrounding David when he wrote this song. It says, "A Michtam of David when Saul sent men, and they watched the house in order to kill him." The king was trying to kill David, but that did not stop David from worshipping God.

> Deliver me from my enemies, O my God;
> Defend me from those who rise up against me.
> Deliver me from the workers of iniquity,
> And save me from bloodthirsty men.
> For look, they lie in wait for my life;
> The mighty gather against me,
> Not *for* my transgression nor *for* my sin, O Lord.
> They run and prepare themselves through no fault of mine.
> Awake to help me, and behold! (vv. 1–4).

> But You, O Lord, shall laugh at them;
> You shall have all the nations in derision.

I will wait for You, O You his Strength;

For God *is* my defense.

My God of mercy shall come to meet me;

God shall let me see *my desire* on my enemies

(vv. 8–10).

Now remember, David was a part of the government. He had been taken into Saul's house after he killed Goliath. However, the king became angry when the people of Israel began singing that Saul has killed thousands, but David has killed tens of thousands. Filled with demonic jealousy and fits of rage, Saul became focused on one task—killing David.

Even though he was anointed as king, and even though he was a national hero for killing Goliath, David had to detach himself from the government and flee for his life. As he sat down to write Psalm 59, King Saul's trained killers were waiting all around David's house, watching for an opportunity to strike.

Surrounded by danger, David began to worship: *Oh God, I have done nothing to deserve this. I ask you to defend me against these bloodthirsty men. Oh God, my strength, I trust You to defend my life.* David's Godward mindset allowed him to keep his focus on God even in the worst of circumstances. He refused to let the devil take God out of his awareness. David reminded himself, *God is bigger than my giants. He is bigger than my mountains. He is bigger than my enemies. He is bigger than my problems.*

The absolute worst thing we can do is forget that God is with us. Why? Because when we forget that

THE ABSOLUTE WORST THING WE CAN DO IS FORGET THAT GOD IS WITH US.

God is with us, the battle is over. The enemy can easily overwhelm us if we do not keep God in the forefront of our minds. A Godward mindset is a choice we can all make at any given point in time.

What Happens When You Keep Your Mind on God

*You have instant encouragement
and a new perspective.*

A Godward mindset affects every part of your life. Instead of seeing a big devil in everything, you begin to see a big God in everything. God gets bigger, and problems get smaller.

*You develop increased faith
and decreased worries and fears.*

The amount you worship and focus on God will always be in direct proportion to your level of peace versus fear and anxiety. In Isaiah 26:3 God promises to give "perfect peace" to those who keep their minds on Him. Focusing on God feeds your faith and starves your fears.

You find a new way of speaking and acting.

You literally talk according to your perspective. Having a Godward mindset causes us to speak and act by faith, allowing God to intervene and change our circumstances. The writer of Hebrews says,

> Without faith *it is* impossible to please *Him*, for he
> who comes to God must believe that He is, and *that*
> He is a rewarder of those who diligently seek Him
> (Hebrews 11:6).

My dad loved the television show *Hee Haw*. It was a country version of the comedy *Rowan and Martin's Laugh-In*. We always had to watch *Hee Haw*, and one of my favorite parts of the show was the song "Gloom, Despair, and Agony on Me." Here are some of the lyrics,

> Gloom, despair, and agony on me
> Deep, dark depression, excessive misery
> If it weren't for bad luck, I'd have no luck at all
> Gloom, despair, and agony on me[1]

Obviously, I have heard that song more than a few times. But there are people who, without realizing it, sing that song every day. Their perspective is so godless. And I am talking about believers! I am not saying that they do not love Jesus. I am not saying that they do not believe in God or that they are on their way to hell. However, for some people, the devil has so succeeded at removing God from their perspective that their confession is "Gloom, despair, and agony on me . . . deep, dark depression."

Sometimes you ask a person, "How are you doing?" but you dread the answer. Now, I do not want to be a stoic. I do not want to be a person who denies the difficulties I am going through. But I can tell you that when God is with us, it is always a good day. Psalm 118:34 says, "This *is* the day the Lord has made; / We will rejoice and be glad in it." Why? Because our God is with us, and He is bigger than our mountains and bigger than our giants. God is bigger than my problems and bigger than my

---

1. Lyrics by Bernie Brillstein, Frank Peppiatt, and John Aylesworth. Recorded by Buck Owens and Roy Clark, Red Boot Records.

enemies. Yes, I may have problems, but it will be a good day because God is working on my behalf.

You become an encourager to other people.

David was the most inspirational king of Israel. He inspired many men to follow him. Even when his wives and children were taken captive and his city was burned to the ground, David rose up and encouraged those around him. By the way, three chapters later, King Saul dies, and David becomes king, surrounded by the men he encouraged at Ziklag.

The devil wants to use your mouth as a microphone to discourage others. He knows that words are powerful, and just a few words can discourage those around you. What decision will you make? Will you share a bad report or a good report? Will your mouth spread discouragement, or will it be God's microphone to spread encouragement?

No matter who they are, people need encouragement. I have made up my mind that my mouth will be God's microphone to encourage other people. Regardless of my circumstances, I will not let my words overwhelm or discourage anyone.

You destroy the power of the devil
to oppress you in any way.

When you put your eyes on God, the devil loses his power to oppress you mentally, physically, spiritually, and in any other way. The devil cannot harass you any longer.

GOD IS BIGGER THAN MY PROBLEMS AND BIGGER THAN MY ENEMIES.

> Let the saints be joyful in glory;
> Let them sing aloud on their beds.
> *Let* the high praises of God *be* in their mouth,
> And a two-edged sword in their hand,
> To execute vengeance on the nations,
> And punishments on the peoples;
> To bind their kings with chains,
> And their nobles with fetters of iron;
> To execute on them the written judgment—
> This honor have all His saints (Psalm 149:5-9).

God's Word is our two-edged sword (Hebrews 4:12), and with it, we fight against the devil. Praise is one of the most powerful weapons against discouragement. David did not let circumstances keep him from praising God; he chose to praise God in the middle of his problems. That was his secret to encouraging himself in the Lord.

Isaiah 61 talks about the ministry of Jesus. Read what verse 3 says concerning what Jesus came into our lives to do.

> To console those who mourn in Zion
> To give them beauty for ashes,
> The oil of joy for mourning.
> The garment of praise for the spirit of heaviness;
> That they may be called trees of righteousness,
> The planting of the Lord, that He may be glorified.

Zion means the house of God—the place where God's people dwell. *Ashes* means devastation. Your life may have been devastated, but God wants to give you beauty instead of ashes.

Mourning in this verse does not mean only crying. It implies deep grief and loss. *The spirit of heaviness* represents oppression or depression. Discouragement may be a reasonable feeling regarding what you have been through. However, when you let it sit there, it becomes a demonic stronghold in your life.

Thankfully, the Bible says that God gives us a *garment of praise* for the spirit of heaviness. Like any garment, praise is not something you are born with, and you do not naturally wake up wearing it. You have to put it on—every day. When you wake up in the morning, you have to decide, "I am going to praise God today. I am not going to let my mind be godless, dark, overwhelmed, or depressed. No matter what my circumstances are, I am going to praise my God."

That decision terrifies the devil. When we praise God in our circumstances, darkness has to flee. God shows up, and we begin to see the miracles we have been praying for come to life.

We chose our focus, and it decides our disposition in life. We can develop a Godward mindset through prayer, praise and worship, studying the Word, and godly teaching. All of these things put our minds on God, which keeps the devil from doing what he wants to do. Remember, a Godward mindset is the number one key to overcoming discouragement.

WHEN WE PRAISE GOD IN OUR CIRCUMSTANCES, DARKNESS HAS TO FLEE.

Realistic Expectations

The second key to overcoming discouragement is having realistic expectations. Let's use King David as an example.

If I were David and someone came to my house and anointed me as king, I would have gone to bed that night and thought to myself, "Wow! Well, first of all, I deserve it. They have finally recognized who I am. I am sure they will show up in a couple of days with a black limo and drive me straight to Jerusalem. There will be a huge coronation ceremony, and from that day forward they will worship me—and rightly so! After all, I will be the king."

Of course, if David had actually thought that, he would have gotten his heart broken, because that is definitely not what happened. When Samuel anointed David as king, problem after problem after problem began to occur.

Rather than riding in a black limo, David went to the front lines of the battlefield and had to kill a giant because everyone else was too scared to do it. Then King Saul turned against David, chasing him all over Israel and forcing him to take refuge with the Philistines—one of Israel's most hated enemies. Then David's family was kidnapped by the Amalekites, and his own men wanted to kill him.

With such mounting, non-stop problems, how did David avoid being overwhelmed? He knew a secret: *there will be a fight, and then I will win*. David never got overwhelmed with his problems because he not only expected warfare and persecution, but he also expected God to come through for him and for God to prevail over the enemy. Both happened. It was not wishful thinking; it was reality.

There is going to be a fight, and then you are going to win. I promise that if you begin to think this way, you will never again be overwhelmed by discouragement. However, if you do not think this way, I can almost guarantee you will get your heart broken. In John 16:33 Jesus says, "These things I have spoken to you, that in Me you may have peace. In the world you will have tribulation; but be of good cheer, I have overcome the world." Jesus says, *There will be a fight, but you will win.*

The Perspective of Overcoming, Advancing Believers

Expect difficulty, then victory.

Paul writes in Romans 5:3–4, "We also glory in tribulations, knowing that tribulation produces perseverance; and perseverance, character; and character, hope." The apostle says, *There are going to be problems. There are going to be bad times. No matter what, though, God is working for our good, which means victory is assured! Yes, there will be a fight, and yes, we will win.*

David was a person who did not get overwhelmed by the fight, even though it was fight after fight after fight. If I were David, I think I might have asked God, "Could You anoint somebody else next time? Or could You at least send a letter to tell me what I am getting myself into before Samuel shows up and pours oil on me? I mean, really! I would have never signed up for *this.*"

THERE IS GOING TO BE A FIGHT, AND THEN YOU ARE GOING TO WIN.

David did not say any of those things because he understood reality. There will be a fight, but then we will win.

The Perspectives of Overcome, Discouraged Believers

Some Christians seem to be discouraged all the time. Here are two perspectives of people who are chronically discouraged.

Expect victory without difficulty.

> Beloved, do not think it strange concerning the fiery trial which is to try you, as though some strange thing happened to you; but rejoice to the extent that you partake of Christ's suffering, that when His glory is revealed, you may also be glad with exceeding joy (1 Peter 4:12–13).

The apostle Peter is trying to comfort believers in the early church by saying, *Are you going through trouble? Well, join the club. Do not be overwhelmed by the fiery trial that is happening to you. This is something common, and you will win—but there will be a fight.*

Research says the best marriages are those with high expectation combined with a realistic attitude of what it will take to succeed. I like to call these people "tough-minded dreamers."

You may ask, "So what is the number one reason for divorce then?" The answer is *disappointment*. The highest divorce rate is among young people 20 to 25 years old. They get married with incredibly unrealistic expectations, expecting the "happily ever after" fantasy to come true.

That is what happened to Karen and me. When we got married, we were 19 years old, and we knew *nothing*. I just expected that I would have her "trained" in a few days. She was not training well while we were dating, so I thought the answer was full-time training. I told myself, "If I could just have her all day, every day, I think I could get her trained, and things would be good." Over 40 years later, let me tell you something: my wife has trained *me* really well. Early in our marriage, though, I got my heart broken because I had such unrealistic expectations about our relationship.

The devil will fight you for your dream marriage and every other dream you have. Marriage *will* be a battle, and you will have to fight for your promised land, just like the people of Israel did. When Moses sent twelve spies to scout out the land God had promised to the people of Israel as their inheritance, the men came back with good news and bad news. The good news was that the land was everything God had promised—fertile and full of good food. However, the bad news was that there were giants in the land. The people of Israel were so discouraged by the giants that they refused to claim their inheritance.

Today, the devil still uses giants to try to discourage God's people. Satan will put giants in your marriage, family, finances, and every other area of your life in which God wants to bless you. If you are going to enter your promised land, you are going to have to fight.

When you are going to hell, Satan will pretty much leave you alone because he does not want to change anything. But when you turn around and decide that you are going to live for Jesus, you start heading toward your Promised Land. That is when the battle begins.

Satan will put giant after giant in your way. By God's grace, you will kill every giant, and you will claim your inheritance. But there *will* be a fight. Trust me. In every good thing that you will ever do in this life, there will be a fight. If there is no fight, then you are headed in the wrong direction. Don't expect victory without difficulty.

Expect difficulty without victory.

Some people have been beaten down so hard for so long that they have just had the battle beaten out of them. Their expectation is "Life is tough, and then you die," like the bumper sticker.

However, I have a new bumper sticker for you: *Life is tough, and then you win!* Life is a battle, but you can and will win. This is Jesus speaking to Peter in Matthew 16:18–19:

> "And I also say to you that you are Peter, and on this rock I will build My church, and the gates of Hades shall not prevail against it. And I will give you the keys of the kingdom of heaven, and whatever you bind on earth will be bound in heaven, and whatever you loose on earth will be loosed in heaven."

Jesus is talking to Peter, but I think He is also speaking to all of us. If you have ever read stories about

IF THERE IS NO FIGHT, THEN YOU ARE HEADED IN THE WRONG DIRECTION.

Peter in the Bible, you know that this disciple was about as sharp as a biscuit. He certainly had the heart, but it took his brain a while to catch up. I truly believe that the reason God chose him is because if Peter could do it, *anybody* can do it. It encourages me to know that God used somebody like that. If God could use him, He can use all of us.

Peter made all kinds of mistakes just days after Jesus spoke this promise over him. For example, the disciple cussed out a little girl next to a fire to keep her from knowing that he belonged to Jesus. He was a coward before he was filled with the Holy Spirit on the Day of Pentecost, and he made a lot of mistakes. But Jesus still told him, "The gates of hell will not prevail against you." And Jesus says the same thing to you: *the gates of hell will not prevail against you.*

In Luke 10:19 Jesus tells His followers, "I give you the authority to trample on serpents and scorpions, and over all the power of the enemy, and nothing shall by any means hurt you."

Jesus promises that nothing will harm you if you fight. He gives us authority over *all* the power of the enemy. If we do not fight, we will be overwhelmed. If we do fight, "We are more than conquerors through Him who loved us" (Romans 8:37).

Our victory has already been won by the death and resurrection of Christ, but it is appropriated daily by faith as we use His authority to face our issues. God has given you such authority that even the very gates of hell cannot prevail against you if you stand up and fight.

That was true of Peter. He became one of the great fighters for the faith. He was able to face adversity because he knew there would be victory in Jesus. And the same was true of David. David knew there would be a fight. Rather than believing, "There must be something wrong with me because I am in a battle," these men realized that the world was battlefield. They had to choose if they were going to fight, and if so, for whom they were going to fight.

If you find yourself in the midst of a battle, there is nothing wrong with you; rather, there is something right with you. During his overwhelming circumstances, David turned to Abiathar the priest and told him to bring the ephod. He asked God, *Do we fight? Do we go?* And God said, *Go, son. You will win and take back everything.*

David did get everything back—his wives, his children, his property, and the love and loyalty of his men. Three chapters later, he becomes the king of Judah, and in 2 Samuel 5 David finally becomes king over all Israel.

Faith in God's Grace

What qualified David to become the king of Israel? From the outside, the answer is *nothing*. Nothing qualified David to be king. He was only a boy—too young, too small, untrained, and unsophisticated. He did not have a background in government or finance. There was nothing that qualified him *except* that God chose him.

You may say, "Well, David had a heart after God." That is true; he did. But he also had sin in his life. He had problems with lust, pride, and violence. Any one of those could have disqualified him. Only the grace of God qualified him.

In times of difficulty, the devil always tries to convince us that God doesn't love us and because of this we will surely fail. We must remember that it is *only* by God's grace that we can do anything!

Roles Satan Plays to Discourage and Defeat Us

Accuser

Satan accuses us to ourselves and uses every problem or failure in our lives to try to beat us down. He wants to convince us that we are doomed to fail, and he introduces fear by accusing God of not being faithful to His Word.

Condemner

Satan wants us to believe that we are defective. He wants us to think that God cannot use us and does not love us. This is where the enemy uses regret. I believe it is one of the most powerful weapons he has to try to trap us in the past.

Tempter

Satan tries to get us to reject God's plan for our lives and to trade our destinies for lower purposes. He keeps whispering, "Give up and go home!"

Comparer

As I discussed in the chapter on comparison, there are two kinds of comparison. God's version relates to

WE MUST REMEMBER
THAT IT IS ONLY BY
GOD'S GRACE THAT WE
CAN DO ANYTHING!

the changeable aspects of our lives—the areas in which we can develop and grow. For example, we look at the character of Christ and the heroes of the faith and are inspired to become more like them. We want to honor God, so we are wise with our finances, diligent with our work, and faithful to our families.

There is another kind of comparison, though. Satan's version looks at the unchangeable aspects of your life, such as your physical attributes and God-given giftings and abilities. The enemy wants you to compare your life status with that of other people and see how you measure up. This type of comparison is deceptive. It presents false "ideals" to get us to believe that we would be happy if only we had something else. Even if we do get the "something else," though, we will always be discouraged because it will never be enough.

We must reject Satan's accusations and attacks against us. He will always try to make the issue *us*—how good or bad we are—and not about God's grace. Any success we have is only by God's grace, and we must put our faith in Him to succeed.

David had a lot of problems, and he knew he was only qualified by the grace of God. There at Ziklag, David never made the issue about himself. You see, that is how you know whether you are walking in grace or not. Grace is all about God and His goodness. Performance is all about us—how qualified we are and how well we are doing.

When I came into the ministry, I had every wrong expectation and got my heart broken over and over again. I was still living in performance to a great degree. It was something like a point system: "If I do enough good, then I deserve good. If I do something bad, then I deserve bad."

Therefore, I was always trying to do good. I was always trying to pedal hard and be a good pastor, a good preacher, a good this, and a good that. Whenever problems came up, I just pedaled harder. I experienced burnout several times as a pastor because I did not rely on the grace of God. Instead, I tried to do everything myself.

I pedaled and pedaled and pedaled until I woke up morning and decided, "I cannot do this anymore." I remember sitting in my office and telling God, "I cannot pedal anymore, Lord. I do not know what is going to happen." I felt like if I stopped performing and doing everything that I was supposed to do, the world would fall apart. And I thought, "That is fine. I am going to go ahead and let the world fall apart. I just cannot do this anymore."

I really thought the Lord would rebuke me and tell me to keep pedaling and to try harder. His actual response was surprising. The Lord said, "Good! Jimmy, you can rest in My grace. You do not have to pedal, son. All you have to do is just obey."

When David was at Ziklag, surrounded by loss and the threat of being stoned, he did not try to perform. He did not try to give an inspirational speech or prove how resilient he was. Instead, he turned to the priest and said, *Just ask God what we are supposed to do.* Abiathar asked God, and God said, *Fight, son.*

Performance is about me, but obedience and grace are about God. Earlier in this chapter we read from Psalm 59. Saul's men had surrounded David's house to kill him, but David writes, "My God of mercy shall come to meet me" (v. 10).

What does "My God of mercy" mean? It means that I do not deserve to be rescued by God. I do not deserve to be used by God. I do not deserve anything God has. Everything I have is a free gift of His grace. I do not deserve it. The only thing I can do is praise Him and obey Him. I do not have to pedal harder, and I do not have to deserve it.

When everything in your life seems to be falling apart, the devil will always try to make it about you. He will whisper, "You are not doing enough. You are a failure. You have failed so many times. You are defective, and God cannot use you anymore."

How can you defeat the devil when he comes against you with condemnation and accusations? You declare, "I do not have to qualify. The blood of Jesus qualifies me, and I rebuke you in the name of Jesus. You will not make this about me."

I know I am weak. I know I do not know enough. I know I am inexperienced. But I serve a gracious God, and my God of mercy will come. It does not matter if you have made mistakes in your marriage, errors in your finances, or poor decisions in your life. Your God of mercy will come to meet you in the midst of your discouragement. One drop of the blood of Jesus is enough to erase all the things you have done wrong.

EVERYTHING I HAVE IS A FREE GIFT OF GOD'S GRACE.

7

OVERCOMING SICKNESS

IN TALKING ABOUT how we are to be overcomers in life, we must remind ourselves of all that Christ's life, death, and resurrection mean to us. Isaiah 53 is a messianic prophecy that graphically describes Jesus' crucifixion and what it accomplished for our sakes.

> He is despised and rejected by men,
> A Man of sorrows and acquainted with grief.
> And we hid, as it were, *our* faces from Him;
> He was despised, and we did not esteem Him.
> Surely He has borne our griefs
> And carried our sorrows;
> Yet we esteemed Him stricken,
> Smitten by God, and afflicted.
> But He *was* wounded for our transgressions,
> *He was* bruised for our iniquities;
> The chastisement for our peace *was* upon Him,
> And by His stripes we are healed (vv. 3–5).

The word *grief* in verse 3 also means sickness, and the word *sorrows* in verse 4 also means pain. Notice that verse 5 does not say, "We *were* healed" or "We *will be* healed." It says *We **are** healed by the stripes of Jesus.*

We need to understand that we deserve sickness. We deserve death. We deserve every curse in this world. Why? Because regardless of how "good" we are, the Bible says, "All of our righteousnesses *are* like filthy rags"(Isaiah 64:6). We may be good compared to other sinful people, but we are not good compared to God. Our sins brought a deserved curse on us. What all of us really deserve is death and hell.

Jesus, the best Man in the history of the world, did not deserve disease. He did not deserve to be rejected by God. He did not deserve poverty. He did not deserve to be cursed.

On that Friday when Jesus hung on the cross, a divine exchange occurred. He took upon Himself what He did not deserve so that by God's grace, we could get what we do not deserve. Now we live based on the grace of God, which brings every blessing—including healing—into our lives.

Galatians 3:13–14 says,

> Christ has redeemed us from the curse of the law, having become a curse for us (for it is written, "Cursed *is* everyone who hangs on a tree"), that the blessing of Abraham might come upon the Gentiles in Christ Jesus, that we might receive the promise of the Spirit through faith.

Jesus became a curse for us. The Bible also says He became sin. On that Friday, God put all the curse of

JESUS TOOK UPON
HIMSELF WHAT HE DID
NOT DESERVE SO THAT
BY GOD'S GRACE, WE
COULD GET WHAT WE DO
NOT DESERVE.

humanity on Jesus Christ—all the sickness, all the disease, all the poverty, all the rejection, etc. Everything that we deserve was put on Jesus Christ.

As I mentioned before, I really believe that the reason the sky turned black for several hours on that Friday afternoon was that Jesus' suffering was so hideous that God did not want anybody to see it. What Jesus went through on the cross is beyond anything we can possibly comprehend. God took the full fury and wrath of His indignation against us and put it on Jesus.

When Jesus said, "It is finished" (John 19:30), that is exactly what He meant. *It is finished.* The curse is gone. Now the blessing of Abraham has been returned to the Gentiles (which simply means non-Jews).

The Blessing of Abraham

Genesis 24:1 says, "Now Abraham was old, well advanced in age; and the Lord had blessed Abraham in all things." *Blessed in all things.* That is the blessing of Abraham.

Being "kind of" blessed is being *not* blessed. You may say, "Well, I have a lot of money," but you are also sick all the time. What good is your money if you are always sick? Or maybe you are very healthy, but you are broke all the time. What good is your health if you are broke all the time? If you are kind of blessed, you are not blessed. Jesus did not come so we could kind of be blessed and kind of be cursed.

Jesus came so we could live in the total blessing of Abraham. Isaiah says, "The chastisement for our peace was upon Him" (Isaiah 53:5a). The English word *peace* is the Hebrew word *shalom*. Unlike our modern definition ("the absence of conflict"), *shalom* means "total well-being." When a Jew greets you and says "Shalom," what he means is, "May God *totally* bless you."

The Sevenfold Exchange at the Cross

The blessing of Abraham has returned to us because the cross was a curse-for-blessing exchange. Jesus took the total curse on the cross so we could live under the total blessing of God.

Here is the seven-fold exchange that happened on the cross on Good Friday.

1. **Death for Life**

   Jesus died to give us life. He said, "I have come that they may have life, and that they may have *it* more abundantly" (John 10:10). Jesus took death so we could have life.

2. **Sickness for Health**

   "By His stripes we are healed" (Isaiah 53:5b).

3. **Rejection for Acceptance**

   Jesus hung on the cross on a Friday afternoon and said, "My God, My God, why have You forsaken me?" (Mark 15:34). On the cross, God the Father turned His back on Jesus and rejected Him because Jesus became a curse and a sin. Why would God reject

Jesus? Because that is what *we* deserve. Because of our sins, we deserve to be rejected. Rather than God rejecting us, though, He rejected His own Son. Now God promises, "I will never leave you nor forsake you" (Hebrews 13:5). For the rest of your life, God will never reject you, even if you deserve it. Jesus took rejection so we could have acceptance.

4. **Poverty for Prosperity**

   Prosperity is our total well-being. The chastisement for our total well-being was upon Jesus.

5. **Defeat for Victory**

   Jesus was defeated. The Romans and the Jews defeated Him and put Him on the cross so we could have victory.

6. **Bondage for Freedom**

   Jesus was bound and taken to the cross so we can be free.

7. **Punishment for Peace**

   God took the full fury of His wrath out on Jesus, and now we can live with the peace of God in our lives as His favored children—His adopted sons and daughters in full standing.

———————

We must know and remember these things because they are our birthright in Christ. The full blessing of God has been returned to us. We no longer live under the curse of the law. We live under the blessing of grace.

WE NO LONGER LIVE
UNDER THE CURSE
OF THE LAW. WE LIVE
UNDER THE BLESSING
OF GRACE.

Here is a wonderful truth: God heals today! *By His stripes we are healed*. However, God does not use a cookie cutter, one-size-fits-all formula. God heals each of us on an individual basis as we put our faith in Him and respond to Him obediently.

Establishing a Scriptural Foundation for Healing Today

If God still heals today, then the Bible is going to confirm that clearly —and it does!

In addition to Isaiah 53, let's look at several passages that address healing.

In John 14:12–14 Jesus says,

> "Most assuredly, I say to you, he who believes in Me, the works that I do he will do also; and greater *works* than these he will do, because I go to My Father. And whatever you ask in My name, that I will do, that the Father may be glorified in the Son. If you ask anything in My name, I will do *it.*"

Notice that Jesus did not say, "You better get all the healing you can get now because when I am gone, the healing is going to go with Me." That is not what He said. No, Jesus promised, *When I leave, you will do greater things than this. Even greater healings will take place through my Church than have taken place through Me.*

In 1 Corinthians 12:7–9 the apostle Paul writes,

> The manifestation of the Spirit is given to each one for the profit *of all:* for to one is given the word of wisdom

through the Spirit, to another the word of knowledge through the same Spirit, to another faith by the same Spirit, to another gifts of healings by the same Spirit.

One of the most common gifts of the Spirit invested in the body of Christ is "gifts of healings." If you will believe it and pray for other people, God would heal others through you. Healing is something that God has invested in His body so we can heal ourselves. Like your body heals itself, the body of Christ also heals itself.

Jesus says in Mark 16:17–18,

> "These signs will follow those who believe: In My name they will cast out demons; they will speak with new tongues; they will take up serpents; and if they drink anything deadly, it will by no means hurt them; they will lay hands on the sick, and they will recover."

When Jesus says, "They will take up serpents," He does not mean you should literally pick up snakes. If you pick up a poisonous snake and get bitten, you will probably die. What this Scripture actually means is that in the unlikely event that a serpent bites you, God will protect you.

The Bible clearly says that healing is a sign that will happen in and through the lives of believers. We must believe this and put our faith in God's Word. However, God does not heal all people the same way.

Why Isn't Everyone Healed?

If Jesus came to take away our sicknesses, then why are some people *not* healed? Why is not everyone healed if this is something that God wants to do? After all, Matthew 8:16–17 says,

> When evening had come, they brought to Him many who were demon-possessed. And He cast out the spirits with a word, and healed all who were sick, that it might be fulfilled which was spoken by Isaiah the prophet, saying:
> "He Himself took our infirmities
> And bore *our* sicknesses."

It says here that Jesus healed everyone. And in Matthew 12:15 we read, "Great multitudes followed Him, and He healed them all." Some people read these Scriptures and say, "Since Jesus healed *everybody*, everybody should be healed."

I agree that everyone "should" be healed, but actually Jesus did *not* heal everybody. When He came to Nazareth, His hometown, Jesus "could do no mighty work there, except that He laid His hands on a few sick people and healed *them*. And He marveled because of their unbelief" (Mark 6:5–6). Jesus heals people of faith in an atmosphere of faith, but He cannot heal where there is no faith.

You may ask, "Does God want to heal everybody?" Absolutely. I believe that if you have faith in God, God will heal you. However, we must understand that one of the main reasons why healing often does not happen

JESUS HEALS PEOPLE
OF FAITH IN AN
ATMOSPHERE OF FAITH,
BUT HE CANNOT HEAL
WHERE THERE IS
NO FAITH.

today is because we have such low expectations. We do not expect God to heal. If you do not expect God to heal, He does not heal. The people of Nazareth had no faith in Jesus, so He could do no mighty miracles. However, when Jesus went out into the wilderness, many people followed Him and put their faith in Him. *All* of them got healed. God wants to heal everybody, but healing requires that we put our faith in Him.

We must also recognize that healing is not always the same. God heals in different ways. Jesus healed some people by laying His hands on them. He healed others by just speaking a word. One day, Jesus healed a man by spitting in the dirt, making mud out of it, and rubbing it on a man's eyes. He healed another man by telling him to dip himself in a pool. Jesus healed Peter's mother-in-law by rebuking her fever. He healed others by casting out demons, and He sent some to show themselves to the high priest.

The bottom line is God still heals today. However, it is a personal issue. Healing is based on our individual faith in Him for grace wherever we are in our own circumstances. God does want to heal you, but He wants to heal you in a personal way.

Six Reasons for Sickness

How does God heal? Well, in part it depends on the reason why we are sick. Just as there are different reasons why we become sick, there are different ways that God heals us. Here are six major reasons for sickness.

Poor Diet and Lifestyle

God wants us to live in a reasonable manner, and if our lifestyle and diet are poor, we are just going to be sick more often.

I once heard a health expert say, "If you show me your diet, I will predict your diseases." He was not a self-righteous guy; he was just stating the obvious. If you eat a lot of sugar or processed foods, you are going to have more illnesses. You are much more likely to have stomach and intestinal problems because of your diet.

If you do not eat foods rich in fiber, like fruits and vegetables, you will experience more sickness. Many of the diseases we suffer from in America are much less common in other areas of the world. Why? Because they eat better than we eat. Likewise, we can see why there is so much sickness in regions of poverty—people simply cannot get adequate nutrition.

One of the most healing foods in the world is water. Our bodies are mostly made up of water, and we need to take in a lot of water every day. However, there are people who spend all day with a giant-sized Coke in their hand. Have you seen those people walking around? Instead of a straw, they have an IV. They sip on sugar all day long!

I am not against drinking carbonated beverages. I do not believe we should be legalistic about that kind of thing. But if all you drink is sugar-filled drinks or coffee, you are going to increase your chances of having certain diseases. Your body needs water to be healthy.

Another lifestyle issue is stress. Stress is currently the number one reason why Americans go to the doctor. In 1967 two psychiatrists, Dr. Thomas H. Holmes and Dr. Richard H. Rahe, published a now famous study on the effects of stress on American life. The Holmes-Rahe Stress Test measures the stress on an individual based on the occurrence of certain events in life. The psychiatrists studied thousands of people and found that the more stress a person had in his or her life, the more likely this person was to become sick and have accidents.[1] You can still take the test yourself online. There is a strong correlation between stress and sickness. We are not designed to live under stress.

When I was a child, I never had the measles, mumps, chicken pox, or any major illness. I had my first cavity when I was 57 years old. My mother used to sit me near sick people all the time, trying to get me to catch stuff so I could develop my immune system. Even though I sat with sick people, I almost never got sick. In fact, it seemed as if I could not get sick, but then I came into the ministry.

When the stress of the ministry came on me, my body fell apart. One Scripture I used to scoff at was Matthew 11:30, in which Jesus says, "My yoke *is* easy and My burden is light." One day I was really under the

---

1. "Social Readjustment Rating Scale" by Thomas Holmes and Richard Rahe. This scale was first published in the *Journal of Psychosomatic Research*, no. 2 (1967): 214.

stress of ministry, and I was having all kinds of physical issues. I said to the Lord, "Your yoke is not easy." And He said to me, "That is not *My* yoke."

I was the one creating the stress by going too fast, doing too much, and consuming a poor diet. When you do those things, you will get sick. God did not design us to live under stress, and He will not give us grace to live under it for long. Of course, He can heal us, but we must be diligent to take care of the bodies He has given to us.

Genetics

We all have predisposed genetic tendencies. If you inherited good genes from your family, that is a blessing. Thank God for good genetics. However, some genetic tendencies go deeper than genes; they reach back to our ancestors' sins that have introduced generational curses upon us.

Nobody wants to pass sickness and disease on to generation after generation. But some of you have inherited a genetic predisposition toward certain illnesses. In fact, some of you may feel like you are a walking time bomb because of what you know is genetically true about your family. You cannot convince me, though, that it is God's will that we would pass diseases from generation to generation.

I have a good doctor. He was my father's doctor, and he also cares for both of my brothers and my son. At my annual physical, my doctor will say, "You know, Jimmy, because of your family, you have this disposition . . ." In a moment, I will tell you how I respond to that.

GOD DID NOT DESIGN US TO LIVE UNDER STRESS.

First, though, let's read Deuteronomy 5:7–10.

"You shall have no other gods before Me.

You shall not make for yourself a carved image—any likeness *of anything* that *is* in heaven above, or that *is* in the earth beneath, or that *is* in the water under the earth; you shall not bow down to them nor serve them. For I, the LORD your God, *am* a jealous God, visiting the iniquity of the fathers upon the children to the third and fourth *generations* of those who hate Me, but showing mercy to thousands, to those who love Me and keep My commandments."

It is true that we inherit our genes. Some of our genes are bad, and in some cases, they are devastatingly bad. A good doctor will tell you that you are genetically predisposed to something because of your genes.

Don't just consider *if* your bad genes are true; consider *why* they are true. Ask yourself, "Why is it true that I have these bad genes in my family?" It brings up an important question: Was there sin back there somewhere?

I believe that the curse of sin can be disease. God says *I am a jealous God, and I visit the iniquity of the fathers generationally.* We know that this is true. Obviously, there was sin involved somewhere back in all of our families.

Then there is another question: What can I do about it? Well, you can do a lot about it.

The first thing is to pray that in the name of Jesus, God will forgive that sin and break the generational curse over your family.

Next, break the bloodline of all your ancestors who went before you. Jesus' sacrifice on the cross has removed the curse of a polluted bloodline and given us access to the bloodline of Abraham, one we should have been a part of since the beginning.

Physically speaking, Jews are genetically linked to Abraham. They do not have to receive the blessing of Abraham; they already have it. But because sin entered the world, we Gentiles (non-Jews) did not have the bloodline of Abraham until Jesus died on the cross. Now, by faith, we can stop all generational curses of sickness and disease. All we have to do is receive our new bloodline in the name of Jesus.

So when my doctor tells me about my genetic predisposition, I just smile at him and think, "In the name of Jesus, I break that right now. I do not accept that I am genetically predisposed to anything. I have a new bloodline." When I leave the doctor's office, I think, "My dad might have had it, my granddad might have had it, and my great-granddad might have had it. But I am *not* going to have it. My son is not going to have it, my grandson is not going to have it, and the rest of our generations are not going to have it. It stops right here in the name of Jesus."

Demonic Strongholds and a Spirit of Infirmity

As I said, God heals in different ways because we are sick for different reasons. Not all sickness is demonic, but some sicknesses are related to a spirit of infirmity. Luke 13:10–16 is an example of a demonic stronghold.

> Now He [Jesus] was teaching in one of the synagogues on the Sabbath. And behold, there was a woman who had a spirit of infirmity eighteen years, and was bent over and could in no way raise *herself* up. But when Jesus saw her, He called *her* to *Him* and said to her, "Woman, you are loosed from your infirmity." And He laid *His* hands on her, and immediately she was made straight, and glorified God.
>
> But the ruler of the synagogue answered with indignation, because Jesus had healed on the Sabbath; and he said to the crowd, "There are six days on which men ought to work; therefore come and be healed on them, and not on the Sabbath day."
>
> The Lord then answered him and said, "Hypocrite! Does not each one of you on the Sabbath loose his ox or donkey from the stall, and lead *it* away to water it? So ought not this woman, being a daughter of Abraham, whom Satan has bound—think of it—for eighteen years, be loosed from this bond on the Sabbath?"

You may ask, "How do I know if I have a spirit of infirmity?" A spirit of infirmity does not respond to medication. Instead of having an occasional sickness, a person with a spirit of infirmity is *always* sick. The woman Jesus healed had been sick for *18 years*.

A spirit of infirmity is a demon. You cannot educate a demon. You cannot disciple a demon. You cannot medicate a demon. The only thing you can do is cast the rascal out.

Sometimes we are sick because we simply have physical issues; there might be nothing spiritual or demonic about it at all. But if you find yourself always sick, always fighting disease, and never getting better, it is worth taking a closer look to see if you may be dealing with a spirit of infirmity.

Sin and Lack of Spiritual Connection and Covering

> Now there is in Jerusalem by the Sheep *Gate* a pool, which is called in Hebrew, Bethesda, having five porches. In these lay a great multitude of sick people, blind, lame, paralyzed, waiting for the moving of the water. For an angel went down at a certain time into the pool and stirred up the water; then whoever stepped in first, after the stirring of the water, was made well of whatever disease he had. Now a certain man was there who had an infirmity thirty-eight years. When Jesus saw him lying there, and knew that he already had been *in that condition* a long time, He said to him, "Do you want to be made well?"
>
> The sick man answered Him, "Sir, I have no man to put me into the pool when the water is stirred up; but while I am coming, another steps down before me."
> (John 5:1–7).

Bethesda means "house of mercy." This man had been sick for 38 years. The expected life span at that time

A SPIRIT OF INFIRMITY IS A DEMON. THE ONLY YOU CAN DO IS CAST THE RASCAL OUT.

was perhaps 40 years, so he would have been considered an old man. He may have been struck ill as a child and suffered for most of his life. We don't know the specific nature of this man's infirmity, but he needed help to get into the pool. Perhaps he was paralyzed.

Jesus walks up and asks him a pretty simple question: *Do you want to get well?* It would seem obvious that a sick person would want to get well, but there are some sick people who do not want to get better because their sickness gives them a ticket out of responsibility. They do not have to work. They do not have to take care of other people. They see themselves only as a victim. They get their medication and live the way they live, and they do not really want to be made well.

The man had been sick for 38 years, but instead of answering, "Yes! I want to get well!" he skirts Jesus' question. He complains about his condition and blames others rather than taking any responsibility. There is definitely something wrong with this man that is deeper than a physical issue.

Ask yourself, "Do I want to get better? Do I want to be made well?" If you want to be made well, God can heal you of any sickness or disease. But we must ask ourselves what we really want. Some people become attached to the identity of their sickness and embrace it. It is the reason they stay sick.

Let's continue with the sick man's story.

> Jesus said to him, "Rise, take up your bed and walk." And immediately the man was made well, took up his bed, and walked.

And that day was the Sabbath. The Jews therefore said to him who was cured, "It is the Sabbath; it is not lawful for you to carry your bed."

He answered them, "He who made me well said to me, 'Take up your bed and walk.'"

Then they asked him, "Who is the Man who said to you, 'Take up your bed and walk'?" But the one who was healed did not know who it was, for Jesus had withdrawn, a multitude being in *that* place. Afterward Jesus found him in the temple, and said to him, "See, you have been made well. Sin no more, lest a worse thing come upon you."

The man departed and told the Jews that it was Jesus who had made him well (John 5:8–15).

This man was in sin. We do not know what his sin was, but we can assume that it was serious based on his condition. Jesus finds him and says, *Listen, you have been made well. Stop that sin, or something worse will happen to you.*

If you are a believer, you are under grace. You do not have to worry that you are going to get sick every time you sin. That kind of thinking is bondage. However, we do have to remember that we have been commanded by God to love each other and walk in grace.

All of us sin, and we need to keep short accounts with God. We need to pray every day and ask the Lord to forgive us. We need to repent, which means taking steps of good faith not to continue in the same sins. When we chronically allow sin into our lives and refuse to repent, we lose God's protective covering and expose ourselves to all kinds of problems.

Romans 6:23 says, "The wages of sin *is* death, but the gift of God *is* eternal life in Christ Jesus our Lord." When we sin and do not repent of it, we open the door for death to come into our relationships, our minds, and our bodies. Wherever sin exists, death comes along with it.

In 1 Corinthians 11:29–30 the apostle Paul teaches about taking communion and says, "For he who eats and drinks in an unworthy manner eats and drinks judgment to himself, not discerning the Lord's body. For this reason many *are* weak and sick among you, and many sleep." Paul wants believers to realize that taking communion in God's house without first confessing your sins is very dangerous. It is eating and drinking judgment on yourself. In the early church, many people became weak and sick and some even died because of this problem.

Paul is giving us an important spiritual revelation: Communion is the covenant sign of the New Testament. Communion is so important in our lives, and it is hard to describe just how powerful it is. But there is only one requirement, and that is not perfection. It is just sincere repentance.

The communion juice or wine represents the blood of Jesus. When I hold the cup, I examine my life and my conscience, and I say, "Lord, I pray that You would forgive me of any sin that is in my life. Please forgive me, God. I sincerely repent of any sin." Then I can take

IF YOU WANT TO BE MADE WELL, GOD CAN HEAL YOU OF ANY SICKNESS OR DISEASE.

the cup and the bread, and not only is communion not a judgment against me, but instead it releases the blessings of God in my life.

God is a gracious, forgiving God. He will forgive us of any sin in our lives, but we need to keep short accounts with Him. We need to understand that sin brings death into our lives. That is why we need spiritual connection and covering.

Unto the Glory of God

John 9:1–3 says,

> Now as *Jesus* passed by, He saw a man who was blind from birth. And His disciples asked Him, saying, "Rabbi, who sinned, this man or his parents, that he was born blind?" Jesus answered, "Neither this man nor his parents sinned, but that the works of God should be revealed in him."

The disciples were conditioned to believe that sickness always meant somebody had sinned, but Jesus said this sickness had nothing to do with sin. The man at the pool of Bethesda was sick because of sin. However, this man was sick simply because he lived in a fallen world and something bad happened to him. That is why Jesus said, *God will glorify Himself through this man's sickness.*

Sometimes there is no reason for sickness other than for God to reveal Himself in a personal and powerful way to a person or group of people.

Unto Death

Sometimes we get sick because we are going to die. My dad died of cancer a number of years ago. He had 6 cancers over a period of 20 years. When he got the first cancer, it was not unto death. He fought it, and we all had faith. I had faith praying for my dad that the Lord would heal him of that cancer, and He did. But 20 years later, when my dad got lung cancer and then leukemia and bone cancer, the day came that we knew this sickness was unto death.

The Lord did heal my dad; He just healed him in a different, eternal way. Unless we are alive when Jesus returns, we will all someday have a sickness unto death.

Psalm 116:15 says, "Precious in the sight of the Lord / *Is* the death of the saints." God does not look at death the same way we do. God looks at death as a homecoming and a graduation. Yes, we want to live long and blessed lives, but there will come a day when the Lord will take us to be with Him.

How God Heals

There are certainly miracles of healing that take place instantly and spontaneously. However, this section deals with how God heals in other ways. Healing is something that takes place gradually; it may be a few days, weeks, or months.

When we pray to the Lord for healing, we need to be sensitive and remember that He works in different ways. Part of your sickness could be related to genetics, lifestyle, or other reasons. Understanding the problem requires some discernment.

Proper Diet, Exercise, and Lifestyle

Probably all of us have some aspects of our lifestyle that contribute to sickness.

The reason that God sometimes heals us gradually is because He wants us to learn a new way of living and a new way of walking. He wants us to confess, believe, and let food, water, and proper nourishment heal our bodies every day.

Most of the cells in your body will die and regenerate themselves regularly. That may take a few days to a few years. Therefore, regardless of how bad off you may be right now, much of your body can regenerate itself. It is a powerful thing that God can do through proper nutrition and lifestyle.

Forgiveness and Walking in Grace

Luke 6:35–36 says,

> "Love your enemies, do good, and lend, hoping for nothing in return; and your reward will be great, and you will be sons of the Most High. For He is kind to the unthankful and evil. Therefore be merciful, just as your Father is also merciful."

Notice that the flow of God's grace in our lives is conditional upon us acting like God and extending grace to others. God promises that as we give grace, it will be returned to us many times over in blessings from Him.

WHEN WE COME INTO
THE BODY OF CHRIST,
WE JOIN THE FLOCK AND
HAVE THE PROTECTION
OF THE GOOD SHEPHERD.

Additionally, we must repent and ask for God's forgiveness for doing anything we know is sinful. Sin exposes us to death, and when we repent, we open the door for God to extend grace and healing to us.

Spiritual Covering and Connection to the Body of Christ

It is not just a convenient, optional thing to come to church. It is essential for every believer to be a part of the body of Christ and be submitted to spiritual leadership. Why? Because we all need spiritual covering.

> Is anyone among you suffering? Let him pray. Is anyone cheerful? Let him sing psalms. Is anyone among you sick? Let him call for the elders of the church, and let them pray over him, anointing him with oil in the name of the Lord. And the prayer of faith will save the sick, and the Lord will raise him up. And if he has committed sins, he will be forgiven. Confess *your* trespasses to one another, and pray for one another, that you may be healed. The effective, fervent prayer of a righteous man avails much (James 5:13–16).

The devil is always looking for the lone sheep. He is always prowling to find someone who is all alone and unprotected. When we come into the body of Christ, we join the flock and have the protection of the Good Shepherd and the spiritual covering of our brothers and sisters in faith.

If there is a sin in your life, you need to confess that sin and then ask for prayer for your sickness. The verses above promise that if we confess our faults to one another and pray for one another, we can be healed. I believe that spiritual covering is essential to keeping us blessed and protected.

Doctors and Medicine

I believe in medical experts and medicine, with one caveat—when I get sick, or when anyone in my family gets sick, the first thing we do is pray and believe God for healing.

I have no hesitation in going to a doctor, chiropractor, therapist, or any other medical specialist. I absolutely believe in those kinds of people, and they have been a big blessing to our lives.

Doctors are trained in a certain way. A doctor can tell you something that is medically true, but this information may not be spiritually true. If you are not careful, it can literally become a curse over your life. Let me give you an example of this.

There was a couple in my church who came down for prayer one day because their grandson was going in to have surgery.

They said to me, "Pastor Jimmy, he has cystic fibrosis. He is going to have this surgery, and he will get pneumonia. It is not the surgery that we are concerned about—it is the pneumonia. The pneumonia could kill him."

I said, "What do you mean he is going to get pneumonia?"

They said, "Well, the doctor told us that kids with cystic fibrosis always get pneumonia when they have this surgery. That is the danger."

I told them, "God bless your doctor. He is being a good
doctor by telling you what he knows to be medically
true, but let us believe something different for just a
minute. Let us believe that your grandson is not going
to get pneumonia."
Their grandson did *not* get pneumonia. He came through
the surgery without any problems, and he was the first
patient the doctor knew of who did not get pneumonia
afterward.

Sometimes we just accept things that are said to
us instead of looking for other solutions, like when
my doctor tells me that I am genetically predisposed
toward a certain disease. He is being a good doctor. He
is not lying; he is telling me from his experience what
is medically true. However, there is a greater truth, and
that is what is spiritually true. What God says is more
true than what any doctor says. I love doctors, and I
appreciate them, but they are not God. When it comes to
the truth, the overarching authority in my life is God.

I do believe in medicine. I especially believe in
medicine that heals, but you have to be so careful of the
medicine that you take. If you see the drug ads on TV,
the side effects may include all kinds of things. I was
watching one day and saw one drug's side effects may
include sudden death. It's hard to get much worse than
that! We need to be very careful about the medications
we use.

I take cholesterol medicine because I have high
cholesterol. When I started taking my first cholesterol
medicine, which was just a tiny pill, Karen noticed that I

WHAT GOD SAYS IS MORE TRUE THAN WHAT ANY DOCTOR SAYS.

began acting differently. I became irritable and grouchy; I was on edge all the time. My doctor told me that this was one side effect of the medication, so he gave me another one. It had the same effect. He tried other options. Finally, the fifth medication I tried worked properly, and Karen said I was back to my normal self again.

You have to be careful of medication because medication has side effects. Take as little medication as you possibly can and absolutely believe God for healing. Remember, medicine is one of the ways God heals, but it is not the only way.

Prayer, Meditation Upon the Word, and Confession

It is amazing what you find when you read the Word of God.

> He sent His word and healed them,
> And delivered *them* from their destructions
> (Psalm 107:20).

Do not sit around talking about your sickness, and do not sit around glorying in your sickness. Instead, confess healing over your body. Find Scriptures about healing and then meditate on those Scriptures. Rebuke pain, speak health, and pray over your body. The Lord wants to heal you, and He heals in an environment of prayer and meditation on His Word.

You may know that anytime a clinical study is performed on medication, doctors always use two things: the actual medicine and the placebo. The placebo looks just like the medicine, but it does not contain any active substances. Often, it is made of sugar or starch. Half the study's participants get the medicine, and the other half get the placebo, but none of the participants know which one they receive.

Even though the placebo is just an inactive pill, there is often a large percentage of the placebo group that still gets healed. How is this possible? Their minds tell them that they are taking medication, and their bodies begin to heal themselves.

Many times, there is also a control group who take nothing at all, and their healing rate is higher as well. It is amazing what the human mind can do when it is thinking correctly.

In Mark 11:23–24 Jesus says,

> "Whoever says to this mountain, 'Be removed and be cast into the sea,' and does not doubt in his heart, but believes that those things he says will be done, he will have whatever he says. Therefore I say to you, whatever things you ask when you pray, believe that you receive *them*, and you will have *them*."

When your mind is thinking positive thoughts and meditating on the Word of God, healing is often a result.

Taking Authority Over the Devil

If your sickness is a spiritual issue, then you need to take spiritual authority. Luke 10:19 says, "I give you the authority to trample on serpents and scorpions, and

IF YOUR SICKNESS IS A SPIRITUAL ISSUE, THEN YOU NEED TO TAKE SPIRITUAL AUTHORITY.

over all the power of the enemy, and nothing shall by any means hurt you."

Do not accept sickness and disease. Fight it by faith! Claim your birthright as a son or daughter of God. If you are constantly sick, take authority over the spirit of infirmity by first exposing it and then refusing to allow it to remain a single moment longer.

Why God Heals

Now that we know some of the different ways God heals, I quickly want to address *why* God heals. I believe there are two main reasons.

1. **We are God's children, and He loves us more than any earthly father has ever loved his children.**
   What earthly father would not want his children to be healthy and happy?
2. **Jesus experienced more sickness than any person in human history.**
   He knows the torment and misery of sickness and does not want anyone to have to endure the curse of it.

Jesus bore our sicknesses so we do not have to. His sacrifice on the cross defeated the devil, paid for our sins, and removed the curse of sin from us. By His stripes we are healed!

8

OVERCOMING DOUBT

THE APOSTLE JOHN records a well-known event in
John 20:19–29.

> Then, the same day at evening, being the first *day* of the
> week, when the doors were shut where the disciples were
> assembled, for fear of the Jews, Jesus came and stood in
> the midst, and said to them, *"Peace be* with you." When
> He had said this, He showed them *His* hands and His
> side. Then the disciples were glad when they saw the
> Lord.
>
> So Jesus said to them again, "Peace to you! As the
> Father has sent Me, I also send you." And when He
> had said this, He breathed on *them,* and said to them,
> "Receive the Holy Spirit. If you forgive the sins of any,
> they are forgiven them; if you retain the *sins* of any, they
> are retained."
>
> Now Thomas, called the Twin, one of the twelve, was
> not with them when Jesus came. The other disciples
> therefore said to him, "We have seen the Lord."
>
> So he said to them, "Unless I see in His hands the
> print of the nails, and put my finger into the print of the
> nails, and put my hand into His side, I will not believe."

And after eight days His disciples were again inside, and Thomas with them. Jesus came, the doors being shut, and stood in the midst, and said, "Peace to you!" Then He said to Thomas, "Reach your finger here, and look at My hands; and reach your hand *here,* and put *it* into My side. Do not be unbelieving, but believing."

And Thomas answered and said to Him, "My Lord and my God!"

Jesus said to him, "Thomas, because you have seen Me, you have believed. Blessed *are* those who have not seen and *yet* have believed."

Thomas is one of the most unfortunate disciples. Every time we hear his name, we think of the word "doubt," thanks to the verses we just read. Even though Jesus spoke about his resurrection to the disciples many times prior to His death, and even though the other disciples tried to convince him, Thomas refused to believe without hard proof.

Here is the good news: Thomas overcame his doubts. He eventually went to India and preached the gospel there. Today, there are many believers in India as well as a shrine to this disciple. Thomas was ultimately martyred by spears for his faith there. Though he doubted at first, he did not remain a doubter. On the contrary, Thomas was a great man of faith who changed nations through his ministry.

All the Disciples Doubted

Thomas is well-known for doubting, but he was certainly not the only one who struggled to have faith. The other disciples doubted too. The above account is in John's gospel, and John mentions Thomas more than the other writers of the gospels do. But listen to what Luke says about Easter Sunday.

> Now as they said these things, Jesus Himself stood in the midst of them, and said to them, "Peace to you." But they were terrified and frightened, and supposed they had seen a spirit. And He said to them, "Why are you troubled? And why do doubts arise in your hearts? Behold My hands and My feet, that it is I Myself. Handle Me and see, for a spirit does not have flesh and bones as you see I have."
>
> When He had said this, He showed them His hands and His feet (Luke 24:36–40).

All of the disciples doubted, not just Thomas. They were *all* "terrified and frightened." Jesus said, *Why do you doubt? Come and touch Me*. The other disciples had to touch Jesus the same way Thomas did.

Jesus appeared to His disciples several times after the resurrection. After these appearances, Matthew 28:16–17 says, "Then the eleven disciples went away into Galilee, to the mountain which Jesus had appointed for them. When they saw Him, they worshiped Him; but some doubted."

Is that not amazing? I am quite sure most of us would think to ourselves, "If I had been there on Resurrection Sunday, and if I had seen and touched Jesus, all my doubts would have been totally resolved." But that is simply not true. The disciples were there. They saw and touched Jesus after the resurrection, but they still doubted.

All of Us Have Doubts

Here is the truth: everyone doubts at some point. It is a human issue. All of us have doubts.

The word *doubt* means "to hesitate" or "to have a lack of conviction about something." In the Bible, the English word *doubt* comes from the Greek word *distazo,* which literally means "two ways." This gives a picture of a person who is standing at a crossroads and hesitating about which of the two ways to go.

Faith means that there is God's way, and because I believe God's way, there is only one way I am going to follow. I just see one thing. I have completely resolved my doubts and now look solely at God's way.

Doubt means that God says something, but people say something else. God says something, but circumstances say something else. God says something, but my past says something else—something that would take me in the other direction. The Word of God says something, but there are skeptics, unbelievers, atheists, and others who refuse to believe. Doubt means I am standing between two ways, literally having "double vision." I

EVERYONE DOUBTS AT SOME POINT. IT IS A HUMAN ISSUE.

hesitate because I lack conviction. I cannot make up my mind between these two directions.

Thomas was a doubter on the day of the resurrection. When the other disciples told him that Jesus was risen from the dead, he hesitated in his belief. He wrestled with the issue until he had proof.

As we just read in Matthew 28, the eleven disciples experienced doubt on the mountain when Jesus appeared to them. They worshipped Him, but they still hesitated in their full acceptance of what was happening. Some Bible commentators believe their doubts were not focused on the identity of Jesus but on their own abilities to fulfill their role once Jesus was gone.

Many of the Bible's famous characters who had very powerful encounters with God also doubted. Abraham is known as "the father of the faith," but he and his wife, Sarah, both doubted God's promise that they would have a child in their old age. Instead, they tried to control the situation themselves, and through the maid Hagar, Ishmael was born. Both Abraham and Sarah laughed because they had such a hard time believing that they would have their own child (Genesis 12:17 and 18:12). However, God was true to His word, and they did have a son. They named him *Isaac*, which means "laughter" (Genesis 21:1–7).

King David doubted God's actions when Uzzah was struck dead for touching the ark of the covenant as it was being transported to Jerusalem (2 Samuel 6:6–11). The king was afraid to bring the ark into the City of David, but he soon saw how God blessed the house where the ark was respectfully cared for. King David joyfully brought the ark into the city and honored the Lord with sacrifices, music, and dancing (2 Samuel 6:12–15).

Moses doubted when God wanted to use him to lead the Israelites out of slavery in Egypt. Moses doubted God, and he especially doubted himself (Genesis 3:1–4:17). Moses did lead the Israelites out of Egypt, though, and God performed many signs and wonders.

However, even after they were freed, the people of Israel struggled with doubt. They witnessed the parting of the Red Sea and the miraculous provision of food and water in the wilderness, but they constantly doubted God's intentions and His ability to protect and care for them. They even refused to enter the Promised Land because they did not believe God would help them defeat the land's current occupants (Numbers 13:31–14:10).

One famous New Testament story about doubt is found in Matthew 14. The disciples were on the Sea of Galilee one night when the sea became very turbulent. Then Jesus came toward the boat, walking on the water. The disciples were terrified, but Peter said, "Lord, if it is You, command me to come to You on the water" (v. 28). Jesus told him to come, so Peter stepped out of the boat and began to walk on the water toward Jesus.

However, as he was walking, Peter looked around and saw how boisterous the wind and the waves were. Suddenly, his single vision toward Jesus became *distazo*—double vision—and he began to sink. Then

Jesus reached out His hand and grabbed Peter. Jesus asked, "Oh you of little faith, why did you doubt?" (v. 31). *Why did you have double vision, Peter? Why did you hesitate between these two directions when I told you exactly what to do?*

All of the examples I just named are people who had powerful encounters with God *before* their doubts. Many people who saw, knew, and walked with Jesus still doubted. Why do people doubt so much? Because it is a part of our human condition. Doubting is just something we do, but it is also something we need to overcome because it can create tremendous problems. We need to overcome our doubts to be people of faith.

Three Truths About Doubt

There Is a Difference between Doubt and Unbelief

Henry Drummond said, "Doubt is *can't believe*; unbelief is *won't believe*. Doubt is honesty; unbelief is obstinacy. Doubt is looking for light; unbelief is content with darkness."[1]

Doubts about God occurs when our intellect cannot grasp what is necessary for us to do what God requires of us. We struggle to understand because we want to obey—that is the source of doubt. Throughout our lives, we are going to doubt, but doubt does not make a person an unbeliever. When I doubt, I am trying to believe. Through my intellect, my senses, my experiences, and

1. Henry Drummond, *Addresses by Professor Henry Drummond* (New York and Chicago: Fleming H. Revell Company, 1891), 81.

IF YOU ARE DEALING WITH DOUBT, GOD IS NOT YOUR ENEMY.

my hurts, I am trying to find a place of faith. I am looking for light.

Unbelief, on the other hand, occurs when we refuse to engage our intellect in an honest effort to believe. Unbelief is a refusal of faith. It will not even try. Without making any effort to the contrary, it just declares, "I will not believe."

Jesus Was Always Gracious to Doubters

If you are dealing with doubt, God is not your enemy. He is actually your very best friend.

Jesus never expressed hostility toward those who doubted Him, even though He had many opportunities to do so. He was not hostile toward Nicodemus, the Pharisee who came late at night with sincere questions (John 3:1–21). He was not hostile toward Mary and Martha, who questioned why He did not come in time to heal their brother Lazarus (John 11:17–32).

Jesus was not hostile toward the doubting father whose son was possessed by a demon. He told the man that anything was possible for those who believe. The man was very honest with Jesus and cried out, "Lord, I believe; help my unbelief!" (Mark 9:24).

Regarding His own disciples, Jesus was not hostile toward Peter or Thomas when they struggled with doubt. When Peter began sinking in the Sea of Galilee, Jesus rescued him. When Thomas needed to touch Jesus to believe, Jesus appeared and said,

> "Reach your finger here, and look at My hands; and
> reach your hand here, and put *it* into My side. Do not be
> unbelieving, but believing" (John 20:27).

Jesus did not reject Peter or Thomas for having doubts. In fact, once they resolved their doubts, He used them greatly.

You may have doubts today. That is okay. God is not offended by our questions or struggles of faith. He knows they exist, and He wants to be a part of the process of our doubts becoming faith. However, this will not happen if we try to hide our struggles from Him. Some people feel as though God is going to punish or reject them for their doubts, so they pretend everything is fine.

Please understand this: if you are doubting but you are sincerely seeking God, you have a friend in Jesus. He can handle your doubts. He is not offended or threatened at all by them.

Doubt Itself Is Not Sin

It only becomes sin when it causes us to disobey God.

Doubt must be a short-term issue in our lives. From the time Jesus first appeared after the resurrection to when He reappeared, Thomas experienced eight days of doubt. It may have felt like a long time to this disciple, but the resolution only took just over a week—not eight years or eighty years.

God will always give us an opportunity to address our doubts about Him. If we will honestly face them, we will find a place of faith. However, if we allow our doubts to

GOD IS NOT OFFENDED BY OUR QUESTIONS OR STRUGGLES OF FAITH.

remain in our lives, they will lead us to disobey (or not obey) God, thus causing a breach in our relationship with Him and a compromise of our lives.

Once again, if you have doubts, that is okay. Just make up your mind that those doubts are not going to define your life. Say to yourself, "This is not going to go on for a long period of time. I have real, sincere doubts, but I am not going to let them become a long-term issue that keeps me from doing what God wants me to do in my life."

Three Steps to Overcoming Doubt

Turn Over Your Doubts to God

Doubt is inevitable, but the difference between chronic doubt and temporary doubt is where it is focused. You will never resolve your doubts until you turn them over to God. As we just saw, God can handle our doubts. In fact, He is sympathetic to our doubts and wants to help us resolve them.

Dealing with the Critic

When I had been saved for about a year, I learned how God can help us handle our doubts. At that time, I knew very little about the Bible. I had never studied the Scriptures before getting saved, so I was still a baby Christian.

I worked with a guy whom I really liked. He was a nice guy, but he was also a critic. In fact, he was a very smart critic who had a lot of arguments against the

Bible. As a new Christian, this was kind of my worst nightmare.

Anytime we talked religion at work—which was often because he knew that I was a strong believer—he would very articulately criticize the Bible and everything about Christianity. I just did not know what to say, so he turned his skepticism toward me. He came at me constantly about why God was not real, why Christianity was not right, and why the Bible was false.

That is what prompted me to start studying God's Word. I was not a Christian by religion; I was Christian by relationship. I *knew* Jesus Christ. He lived in my heart, He spoke with me, and there was nothing that you could tell me to convince me He was not real.

Still, it frustrated me that I could not answer my friend. I did not have an intelligent response, and I would leave work sometimes thinking, "You should be able to say something intelligent in the conversation." So I went home and prayed about it. I said, "Lord, help me to respond to him in an intelligent manner and be able to defend my faith in front of him."

As I began to study the Scriptures, I found out that many of the things my friend was saying were simply not true. In fact, everything he was saying was misguided. It was not that he was mean or vicious toward me; he was just talking to me about his honest doubts and skepticism about Christianity.

I made up my mind that I was not going to let this cause me to lose my faith or to have any sincere doubts about God. In addition to reading the Bible, I went to the Christian bookstore in town and asked the owner to help me find books on the questions my friend had. I read books about evolution. I read books about creation science. I read books about everything my friend brought up, and I found answers to every issue he raised. Then I would go back to him, and we would just sit there and talk. Eventually, I got to where I could articulate responses to the things he was saying.

Look: God is always right, and He is never threatened by any information. All honest information points to God. All honest science points to God. Creation declares the glory of God. We do not have to be afraid of anything anyone might say. There is an intelligent response for every question.

I kept coming back to my friend with answers. After a while he knew that I would come back with a response to whatever he said. One day, he came into work looking terrible, as if he had just been through World War III. I asked if he was okay, and he said that he was not. When I asked him what was wrong, he told me his situation, and then he said, "Jimmy, I need Jesus. I need to receive Him in my life. I need to get saved."

I led him in a prayer that morning, and he received Jesus as his Lord. Here is what I want you to understand: when my friend pointed his doubts toward me, I pointed mine toward God, and my faith grew stronger because of it. Somebody will point their doubts toward you someday, and you could be God's voice to that person to help them find faith.

GOD IS ALWAYS RIGHT, AND HE IS NEVER THREATENED BY ANY INFORMATION.

Decide today that you will not let people produce doubts in your life about God. Tell yourself, "I am going directly to God. I am going to find out the truth." Every time I go to God and take my doubts to Him, they are resolved. This happens not by meaningless answers or even just belief. It happens by the truth. Jesus said, "I am the way, the *truth*, and the life" (John 14:6, emphasis mine).

Dealing with the Skeptic

There are many honest questions about God and reality that we will inevitably be confronted with and will need to address.

Tim Keller, the founding pastor of Redeemer Presbyterian Church in New York City, is a wonderful Christian intellectual and apologist. He has dealt with doubters his entire ministry. Being one of the least religious and most skeptical cities in the United States, New York City is sometimes called the "Garden of Doubt."

In 2008 Keller wrote one of the best books available on the topic of doubt and belief. The title is *The Reason for God: Belief in an Age of Skepticism*, and I highly recommend it. In his book, Keller outlines the seven biggest problems skeptics have with Christianity.

1. There can't be just *one* true religion.
2. How could a good God allow suffering?
3. Christianity is a straightjacket.
4. The Church is responsible for so much injustice.
5. How can a loving God send people to hell?

6. Science has disproved Christianity.

7. You can't take the Bible literally.[2]

Keller's book is a fantastic resource that squarely addresses all of these issues with a reasoned response. He takes doubt and turns it toward God to help people with honest questions find faith.

However, even Jesus could not help doubters who would not turn toward God. He could not help the rich younger ruler (Matthew 19:16–22), and He could not help the people of His hometown, Nazareth (Mark 6:4–6). Jesus could not resolve the Pharisees' doubts because so few of the Pharisees believe in Him. And He was not able to help Judas resolve his doubts, which ultimately led to the disciple's betrayal of Jesus for 30 pieces of silver.

There were many people around Jesus who were insincere doubters. They were unbelievers, not even willing to engage in an honest discussion about the reality of God.

Dealing with the Opponent

In 2004 my father-in-law sponsored a debate in New York City between Antony Flew, once the leading atheist in the world, and others, in particular noted apologist Roy Varghese. Varghese is an intellectual who is also a friend of my father-in-law. He loves to get unbelievers and believers together to debate Christianity.

---

2. Timothy Keller, *The Reason for God: Belief in an Age of Skepticism* (New York: Penguin Group, 2008).

A contemporary of C.S. Lewis, Flew was a student and then lecturer at Oxford University in the late 1940s. Flew took classes under Lewis and was a member of the Oxford Socratic Club[3] that Lewis presided over for many years, but Flew himself did not believe in God. In fact, he was a prominent atheist spokesperson for decades.

Not long after the 2004 debate, Flew surprised many people by saying that he now believed in God. He tells the story of this change in the book, *There Is A God: How the World's Most Notorious Atheist Changed His Mind*,[4] which he coauthored with Varghese. The reason that Flew changed his mind is because he was an honest man.

Flew was an atheist, and he said, "Someone will have to explain to me how God can exist before I believe that God will exist." Roy Varghese has lived his life believing that the universe declares the glory of God and that everything demonstrates God's existence. He has dedicated his life to helping people with their doubts, and he found one man, the leading atheist in the world, who was a sincere doubter.

There are some people who are just unbelievers; no matter what you say, they will not believe. But never think that just because a person is a skeptic or a doubter, they cannot be changed—because they can.

3. The Socratic Club was formed at Oxford in 1941 as a forum for debate between atheists and Christians.
4. Antony Flew and Roy Abraham Varghese, *There Is a God: How the World's Most Notorious Atheist Changed His Mind* (New York: Harper Collins, 2008).

Dealing with Tragedy

I have not ministered in a place like New York City and dealt with skepticism the same way Tim Keller has. However, I have spent my entire ministry helping people address their doubts about God, especially related to suffering and loss in their lives. As a pastor, I often deal with people and families who have tough questions.

- Why did God allow my loved one to die? (especially when the death is tragic or untimely)
- Why does God allow me to suffer?
- Why does God not answer my prayers?
- If God loves me as much as He loves others, why am I not as blessed as others?
- Why do I not hear God's voice?

All of those questions are valid, and we need to be honest with God about them. We must not allow our doubts about God to keep us from taking our questions to Him.

God knows when you are hurting. He knows when you are suffering, He knows when events occur that could be interpreted as though He does not care about you, does not love you, or is not protecting you. However, none of those things is true. Do not let your doubts or your pain cause you to turn away from God. Regardless of your circumstances, God does love you.

The devil always wants us to interpret our circum- stances as being God's fault because he wants to damage our relationship with God. About 25 years ago, Karen

WE MUST NOT ALLOW
OUR DOUBTS ABOUT
GOD TO KEEP US FROM
TAKING OUR QUESTIONS
TO HIM.

and I went through the worst season in our lives. During a six-week period of time, we experienced three devastating events, one right after the other.

The first was a personal, devastating issue in my life. The second was the near death of a very close family member, under tragic circumstances. The third event was Karen getting hit by a semi-truck while she was driving in her car.

After preaching one Sunday morning, I went home and took a nap. (Actually, I tell people that I do not "nap" on Sundays—I go into a *coma*.) I was in my Sunday afternoon coma when my son, Brent, ran into the bedroom and woke me up. The police had called our house (this was before cellphones), and when Brent answered, they said, "Your mother has been in a wreck." They told him what happened and where Karen was. Together, we rushed down Interstate 40 to where the wreck had happened. We arrived just as the ambulance was pulling away with Karen, and we followed the ambulance to the emergency room.

The only thing I knew was that my wife had been in a wreck; I did not know any of the details. When they pulled her out of the ambulance, Karen had blood all over her and just looked terrible. She had a big gash on her head, but thankfully she did not have any internal injuries. She was just bruised and cut all over. (Today, Karen cannot remember any of this because the impact of the wreck knocked her out.)

When the nurses took her into the exam room to work on her, I came in right behind them. The doctor said,

"Mr. Evans, you have to go out into the waiting room. You cannot stay in here."

Now my mind was just spinning. This was the third in a series of devastating events in just six weeks. As I walked out of the exam room, I thought, "God must be finished with me." I had no idea what was going to happen to my ministry or my family. Did God still love me? Did He care? Was He against me? Did I do something wrong?

With those thoughts in my head, I walked into the waiting room and stood over in the corner by myself. Right there I said to the Lord, "If You are trying to say something to me, I want You just to say it to me, but please do not kill my family."

Then the Lord replied, as clearly as I have ever heard Him, "I *am* trying to say something to you, Jimmy." And I said, "What?" He replied, "I love you."

To be honest, I thought, "Well, I am glad You do not hate me. You have a funny way of showing love, though." I wondered, "What do You mean You are trying to say that You love me? What do You mean by that?" Because I could not process it.

Nevertheless, I made up my mind right there that I was not going to let this make me turn my heart away from God. It is very easy at times like that to just shake your fist at heaven and say, "Okay, well, if this is the way You are going to be, I can deal with that" and then go and turn your doubts to the bartender, your friends, a psychic hotline, or something else. But I made up my mind: *I am not going to turn away from God. I am going to believe that there is something good in this.*

I can now say, some 25 years later, that the next six months of our lives were about the most glorious six months that we ever experienced. I absolutely believe that God did not *cause* any of those devastating things to happen. However, I am telling you that He took a sow's ear and made a silk purse out of it.

We were showered with love after Karen's wreck. I can't begin to tell you how many cards, flowers, and people came to our house. I gained 20 pounds from all the food people brought. God healed us in the deepest part of our hearts through that circumstance.

The individual in our family who almost died by tragic circumstances got gloriously saved, and all our lives have been dramatically different ever since. Every issue that caused me to doubt God was resolved.

Trust God's Word to Resolve Your Doubts

Romans 10:17 says, "Faith *comes* by hearing, and hearing by the word of God." Turn your doubt toward God and trust His Word—not skeptics or unbelievers—to resolve it.

During his years of earthly ministry, Jesus told the disciples over and over again that He was going to be crucified and resurrected on the third day. In Luke 9:22 Jesus says, "The Son of Man must suffer many things ... and be killed, and be raised the third day."

The problem with Thomas was not that he did not believe the other disciples who saw Jesus after the resurrection; the problem was that he did not believe *Jesus*. Jesus had told him, *I am going to be resurrected on the third day*. When Thomas rejected the news that Jesus was alive, he was rejecting the word that God gave him. He wanted further proof. However, God's Word is the only proof necessary for faith to exist and for doubt to die.

When Peter saw Jesus walking upon the Sea of Galilee, he asked if Jesus wanted him to come, and Jesus said yes. The word of Jesus was all Peter needed to walk on the water. However, the disciple then began to look back and forth between Jesus and the waves. This double vision caused him to reject the Lord's word and begin to sink. That is why Jesus asked, "Why did you doubt?" (Matthew 14:31).

If the words of people or circumstances in your life have as much or more credibility to you than God's Word, your doubts will never be answered. If we are going to settle our doubts, we must come to the point where God's Word to us is the highest standard of truth and the only source of proof necessary for something to be real.

The devil's first words to humans were, "Has God indeed said ...?" (Genesis 3:1). Just as he did with Adam and Eve in the Garden of Eden, the devil always wants us to doubt God's Word so that he can keep us confused, disoriented, and defeated. He especially uses difficulty, suffering, and problems to question God and His Word.

What will resolve your doubts? Will it be the word from an expert who opposes God? Will it be a change

GOD'S WORD IS THE ONLY PROOF NECESSARY FOR FAITH TO EXIST AND FOR DOUBT TO DIE.

in your emotions or your circumstances? We must remember that the Word of God is our sword of the spirit and the source of success in every area of life.

Doubt will be present in almost every circumstance that requires faith in the life of a believer. This includes prayer, giving, spiritual gifts, obedience, etc. The key is to make doubt subject to faith in the Word of God.

Take a Step of Faith and See What Happens

Often I have stood at a place of doubt between two opinions—what I saw or experienced and what God's Word says. As I sit there doubting in those times, the only thing that resolves my doubt is taking a step of faith. Faith is not the absence of doubt. Faith is the overcoming of doubt.

Acting in faith does not mean that you have no doubts; instead, it means your mind is made up. You will not stay in this place of indecision any longer. You have chosen, and you choose God. You have turned your doubt toward God. You will believe the Word of God over everything that anyone else says or what you see, think, feel, or hear. You will step out and do it.

I like to say, "You will doubt it until you do it, and then you won't because you don't." In other words, you will understand after you do what God says and experience the results—but not before!

> The fear of the Lord *is* the beginning of wisdom;
> A good understanding have all those who do *His*
> commandments.
> His praise endures forever (Psalm 111:10).

I have had to take many steps of faith in my life. I heard the gospel growing up, but I doubted it until I gave my life to Christ. Then I never doubted it again.

One day, my friend wanted me to go down to a healing line at camp because I had hurt my arm. I did not want to get in line because I doubted that type of thing, but I went anyway. My arm was healed, and I never doubted healing again.

When Karen and I first heard a pastor preach about tithing, I was very offended at the idea of giving money to a church. But Karen wanted to give. So we did, and God did a miracle in our finances.

God also did a miracle in our marriage. Karen and I had serious marriage problems. I knew what the Bible had to say about marriage, but I doubted it would work for us. On the brink of divorce, I finally obeyed, and God completely transformed our relationship.

My journey of faith is no different from anyone else's journey. We all hear the Word of God and know what we should do, but we doubt. That doubt causes us to have double vision as we consider the different ways for a while. We finally have to come to the point of taking the step of faith away from our doubts toward God. Then and only then is when God reveals Himself and supernaturally resolves all of our doubts.

———————

Hebrews 11:6 says, "Without faith, *it is* impossible to please *Him,* for he who comes to God must believe that

FAITH IS NOT THE
ABSENCE OF DOUBT.
FAITH IS THE
OVERCOMING
OF DOUBT.

He is, and *that* He is a rewarder of those who diligently seek Him." God will not reject us because of our doubts, but He will not reward us until we take the step of faith that acknowledges His presence and His promises.

Some of you have allowed your doubts about God to keep you away from Him or from giving your life totally to Him. God loves you, and He wants to meet you today as your Lord and Savior. He will forgive you for all of your sins, but it will require a response of faith on your part.

Some of you have experienced a problem or loss in your life that has caused you to question God and His love. It is time to come back to God and believe what His Word says. Read Jeremiah 29:11. God's plans for you are *good*, not evil. He loves you and wants to give you a hope and a future.

Some of you have allowed the voices of skeptics or unbelievers to shake your faith and keep you from living fully for God. It is time to make God's Word the standard of truth in your life, not the voices of other people. God's Word is the proof of reality.

May God bless you with an overcoming life.

APPENDIX 1

LEADER'S GUIDE

LEADER'S GUIDE

This Leader's Guide is designed to help you lead your small group or class through *The Overcoming Life*. Use this guide along with the book for a life-changing, interactive experience.

Before You Meet

Ask God to prepare the hearts and minds of the people in your group. Ask Him to show you how to encourage each person to integrate the principles they discover through reading this book and group discussion into their daily lives.

Before the meeting, read the chapter you will be discussing and familiarize yourself with that chapter's discussion and activation questions.

Plan how much time you'll give to each portion of your meeting (see the suggested schedule below).

Suggested Small Group Schedule

- **Engage** and **Recap** (5 Minutes)
- **Read** (20 Minutes)

- **Talk** (25 Minutes)
- **Pray** (10 minutes)

Key Tips for Leaders

- Generate participation and discussion.
- Resist the urge to teach. The goal is for great conversation that leads to discovery.
- Ask open-ended questions—questions that cannot be answered with "yes" or "no" (e.g., "What do you think about that?" rather than "Do you agree?").
- When a question arises, ask the group for their input first, instead of immediately answering it yourself.
- Be comfortable with silence. If you ask a question and no one responds, rephrase the question and wait for a response. Your primary role is to create an environment where people feel comfortable to be themselves and participate, not to provide the answers to all of their questions.
- Ask the group to pray for each other from week to week, especially about key issues that arise during your time together. This is how you begin to build authentic community and encourage spiritual growth within the group.

Keys to a Dynamic Small Group

Relationships

Meaningful, encouraging relationships are the foundation of a dynamic small group. Teaching, discussion, worship, and prayer are important elements of a group meeting, but the depth of each element is often dependent upon the depth of the relationships among members.

Availability

Building a sense of community within your group requires members to prioritize their relationships with one another. This means being available to listen, care for one another, and meet each other's needs.

Mutual Respect

Mutual respect is shown when members value each other's opinions (even when they disagree) and are careful never to put down or embarrass others in the group (including their spouses, who may or may not be present).

Openness

A healthy small group environment encourages sincerity and transparency. Members treat each other with grace in areas of weakness, allowing each other room to grow.

Confidentiality

To develop authenticity and a sense of safety within the group, each member must be able to trust that things discussed within the group will not be shared outside the group.

Shared Responsibility

Group members will share the responsibility of group meetings by using their God-given abilities to serve at each gathering. Some may greet, some may host, some may teach, etc. Ideally, each person should be available to care for others as needed.

Sensitivity

Dynamic small groups are born when the leader consistently seeks and is responsive to the guidance of the Holy Spirit, following His leading throughout the meeting as opposed to sticking to the "agenda." This guidance is especially important during the discussion and ministry time.

Fun

Dynamic small groups take the time to have fun! Create an atmosphere for fun and be willing to laugh at yourself every now and then.

APPENDIX 2

STUDY GUIDE

OVERCOMING REJECTION

Introduction

Rejection may be the most difficult thing for people to overcome. It is both our greatest fear and our greatest scar. However, we are not alone. Jesus was the most rejected human being in the history of the world, and He overcame rejection on the cross. When we put our faith in Jesus, we are accepted forever.

Key Thought

Two thousand years ago, God rejected His Son once and for all so that He will never reject us again in eternity.

Key Scriptures

Isaiah 53:2–3

> For He shall grow up before Him as a tender plant,
> And as a root out of dry ground.
> He has no form or comeliness;

And when we see Him,

There is no beauty that we should desire Him.

He is despised and rejected by men,

A Man of sorrows and acquainted with grief.

And we hid, as it were, *our* faces from Him;

He was despised, and we did not esteem Him.

Hebrews 13:5–6

Let your conduct *be* without covetousness; *be* content with such things as you have. For He Himself has said, "I will never leave you nor forsake you." So we may boldly say:

"The Lord *is* my helper;

I will not fear.

What can man do to me?"

Discussion

- Thinking about the different forms of rejection, which one has most affected you in the past? Does this feeling of rejection still influence your life today?

- Read Mark 15:34. *Forsake* means to renounce or turn away from entirely. Why do you think Jesus made this statement to the Father as He hung on the cross? Is it hard for you to comprehend God forsaking Jesus?

- There are four common yet unhealthy ways to react to rejection: avoidance, anger, hopelessness, and dependency. Which of these has been your most common reaction to rejection, and why do you think you tend to react that way?

Activation

- What person (or people) in your life do you need to forgive for rejecting you?
- Have you ever felt joy at being rejected? Ask God to help you share your faith with someone this week, even if it means possibly being rejected.

OVERCOMING FEAR

Introduction

Jesus experienced more fear than any other human being has ever experienced. He literally took hell upon Himself so we could have heaven. Jesus conquered fear by admitting it without shame, keeping His eyes on the Father, and facing His fear by faith. Jesus is our Prince of Peace, and through Him, we can overcome fear as well.

Key Thought

Jesus can intercede on our behalf as our High Priest in heaven because He experienced the same attacks from the devil that we do.

Key Scriptures

Psalm 16:8–11

I have set the Lord always before me;
Because *He is* at my right hand I shall not be moved.

Therefore my heart is glad, and my glory rejoices;
My flesh also will rest in hope.
For You will not leave my soul in Sheol,
Nor will You allow Your Holy One to see corruption.
You will show me the path of life;
In Your presence *is* fullness of joy;
At Your right hand *are* pleasures forevermore.

Hebrews 4:15–5:1

We do not have a High Priest who cannot sympathize with our weaknesses, but was in all *points* tempted as *we are, yet* without sin. Let us therefore come boldly to the throne of grace, that we may obtain mercy and find grace to help in time of need. For every high priest taken from among men is appointed for men in things *pertaining* to God, that he may offer both gifts and sacrifices for sins.

Discussion

- Read Luke 22:39–47. How does it make you feel to know that Jesus experienced fear before He suffered and died to save you from your sins?
- What is the difference between good fear and bad fear? How do your responses differ between the two?
- How would you counsel another believer who has a fear of death?

Activation

- What personal fear(s) do you need to bring into the light and submit to God?
- What are some ways you can begin to starve your fears and feed your faith?

OVERCOMING COMPARISON

Introduction

Comparison plants negative thoughts about God, ourselves, and others in our minds. It is a curse that keeps us from being the people whom God wants us to be. To overcome comparison, you must keep your eyes on Jesus and embrace your unique calling and destiny.

Key Thought

If you do not let God bless other people the way He wants to bless them, He will not bless you the way you want Him to bless you.

Key Scriptures

Romans 8:5–6

For those who live according to the flesh set their minds on the things of the flesh, but those *who live* according to the Spirit, the things of the Spirit. For to be carnally minded *is* death, but to be spiritually minded *is* life and peace.

James 3:14–16

If you have bitter envy and self-seeking in your hearts, do not boast and lie against the truth. This wisdom does not descend from above, but *is* earthly, sensual, demonic. For where envy and self-seeking *exist,* confusion and every evil thing *are* there.

1 Corinthians 12:12

For as the body is one and has many members, but all the members of that one body, being many, are one body, so also *is* Christ. For by one Spirit we were all baptized into one body.

Discussion

- Read John 21:15–22. Why is loving Jesus first and foremost the most important qualification for ministry?
- How does Jesus feel about comparison? How does comparison affect your relationship with God?
- What is envy, and why is it a boundary violation?

Activation

- Accepting yourself as God's special creation is vital to overcoming comparison. What areas of comparison do you need to address in your life?
- Think about the people whom you impact every day. How can you use your unique gifts to honor and minister to them?

OVERCOMING SHAME

Introduction

God created us to be shameless, but sin causes us to hide from Him and each other. Sin creates shame that damages our self-image and our social and spiritual abilities. On the cross, Jesus completely and eternally defeated sin and shame. In order to live victoriously, we must understand that not only are we forgiven, but our shame is gone too.

Key Thought

When God forgives sin, it is forgotten. He never brings it up a second time, and He never remembers it again for all eternity.

Key Scriptures

Hebrews 12:1–2

Since we are surrounded by so great a cloud of witnesses, let us lay aside every weight, and the sin which so easily ensnares *us,* and let us run with endurance the race that is set before us, looking unto Jesus, the author and finisher of *our* faith, who for the joy that was set before Him endured the cross, despising the shame, and has sat down at the right hand of the throne of God.

Romans 8:1

There is therefore now no condemnation to those who are in Christ Jesus, who do not walk according to the flesh, but according to the Spirit.

Revelation 12:10–11

Then I heard a loud voice saying in heaven, "Now salvation, and strength, and the kingdom of our God, and the power of His Christ have come, for the accuser of our brethren, who accused them before our God day and night, has been cast down. And they overcame him by the blood of the Lamb and by the word of their testimony, and they did not love their lives to the death."

Discussion

- Does God ever use shame in our lives? Why or why not?
- Why did the people of Israel need two goats for the Day of Atonement? How is Jesus our scapegoat?
- What is the difference between confession and repentance? Why are both of these actions important steps toward overcoming shame?

Activation

- What areas of shame do you recognize in your life? Take authority over shame by thanking Jesus for His blood and what He has done for you.
- It is important to forgive those who have shamed or hurt you. What person (or people) in your life do you need to forgive?

OVERCOMING UNFORGIVENESS

Introduction

God takes the issue of unforgiveness very seriously. Jesus suffered and died on the cross to forgive us for all of our sins. His sacrifice is more than we could ever repay. It is ridiculous for us to withhold forgiveness from others in light of God's incredible grace toward us. If we will not forgive others, He will not forgive us.

Key Thought

If you refuse to forgive, you walk out from under God's wings and onto Satan's property. You expose yourself to torture and torment.

Key Scriptures

Ephesians 4:26–27

"Be angry, and do not sin": do not let the sun go down on your wrath, nor give place to the devil.

Matthew 6:15

"If you do not forgive men their trespasses, neither will your Father forgive your trespasses."

Romans 12:17–19

Repay no one evil for evil. Have regard for good things in the sight of all men. If it is possible, as much as depends on you, live peaceably with all men. Beloved, do not avenge yourselves, but *rather* give place to wrath; for it is written, "Vengeance is *Mine*, I will repay," says the Lord.

Discussion

- Unforgiveness affects us in every way. What kinds of physical and emotional problems can be traced back to unforgiveness?
- Why is "conditional forgiveness" not really forgiveness at all?
- How can you forgive someone but still have the right to protect yourself and confront that person?

Activation

- If you struggle with unforgiveness, remind yourself, "I may not have done a particular wrong thing, but I did enough wrong to put Jesus on the cross. I owe Him everything."
- Is there someone you know you should forgive but have trouble doing so? Begin praying blessings for that person today. As you pray for them, you will be healed.

OVERCOMING DISCOURAGEMENT

Introduction

Every person will face discouragement at some point in life. The devil wants us to become so overwhelmed by our circumstances that we do not fulfill God's plan for our lives. However, staying in discouragement is not a condition; it is a choice. We can choose to encourage ourselves in the Lord, just like David did.

Key Thought

God has given you such authority that even the very gates of hell cannot prevail against you if you stand up and fight.

Key Scriptures

Psalm 16:8

I have set the LORD always before me
Because *He is* at my right hand I shall not be moved.

Isaiah 61:3

> To console those who mourn in Zion
> To give them beauty for ashes,
> The oil of joy for mourning.
> The garment of praise for the spirit of heaviness;
> That they may be called trees of righteousness,
> The planting of the Lord, that He may be glorified.

Discussion

- Read Psalm 59:1–4, 8–10. How did David keep a Godward mindset even while King Saul was trying to kill him? Why is forgetting that God is with us the worst thing we can do?
- What "qualified" David to overcome discouragement and be victorious? What qualifies you?
- How are discouragement and comparison related? What are the changeable and unchangeable aspects of your life?

Activation

- Examine your expectations. Are they realistic? Expect difficulty, then victory.
- Ask yourself, "Am I basing my peace on God's grace or my performance?" Remind yourself that everything you have is a free gift of God's grace.

OVERCOMING SICKNESS

Introduction

Jesus took the total curse of sin and sickness on the cross so we could live under the total blessing of God. God does heal today, and Scripture clearly confirms this. However, God does not heal everyone in the same way. Healing is based on our individual faith in Him for grace wherever we are in our own circumstances.

Key Thought

The Lord wants to heal you, and He heals in an environment of prayer and meditation on His Word.

Key Scriptures

Isaiah 53:5

The chastisement for our peace *was* upon Him,
And by His stripes we are healed.

Galatians 3:13–14

Christ has redeemed us from the curse of the law, having become a curse for us (for it is written, "Cursed *is* everyone who hangs on a tree"), that the blessing of Abraham might come upon the Gentiles in Christ Jesus, that we might receive the promise of the Spirit through faith.

Psalm 107:20

He sent His word and healed them,
And delivered *them* from their destructions.

Discussion

- What is the blessing of Abraham, and how did Jesus restore this blessing on the cross?
- If Jesus removed the curse of sickness, why are some people *not* healed?
- How is a spirit of infirmity different from other illnesses? How can you overcome it?

Activation

- Ask yourself, "Are there any aspects of my lifestyle that contribute to sickness?"
- Does your family have any sicknesses that appear generation after generation? If so, refuse to accept that curse any longer. Claim your birthright to the new bloodline you have in Jesus.

OVERCOMING DOUBT

Introduction

Everyone has doubts. Doubts are simply part of the human condition. If you are experiencing doubts, God is not your enemy. He is not offended by your questions or struggles. Instead, God wants to be a part of the process of your doubts becoming faith.

Key Thought

God's Word is the only proof necessary for faith to exist and for doubt to die.

Key Scriptures

Romans 10:17

Faith *comes* by hearing, and hearing by the word of God.

Psalm 111:10

The fear of the Lord *is* the beginning of wisdom;
A good understanding have all those who do *His*
commandments.

His praise endures forever.

Hebrews 11:6

Without faith, *it is* impossible to please *Him*, for he who
comes to God must believe that He is, and *that* He is a
rewarder of those who diligently seek Him.

Discussion

- Many people remember Thomas as the disciple who
  doubted. What other famous biblical characters
  struggled to have faith?
- What is the difference between doubt and unbelief?
  What is the difference between doubt and sin?
- Do you have to be free from doubt to act in faith?
  Why or why not?

Activation

- How should you respond to skeptics and critics
  regarding their doubts about God?
- Are you currently dealing with any of your own
  doubts? If so, take them straight to God and allow
  Him to resolve them.

ABOUT THE AUTHOR

JIMMY EVANS IS the founder and CEO of MarriageToday, a ministry based in Dallas, Texas, that is devoted to helping couples build strong and fulfilling marriages and families. Jimmy and his wife, Karen, are passionate about marriage, and together, they co-host *MarriageToday* at www.marriagetoday.com.

Jimmy also hosts *The Overcoming Life,* a daily television program dedicated to seeing people thrive in life and in their walk with God. He serves as senior pastor at Gateway Church, a multi-campus church in the Dallas/Fort Worth Metroplex, and as an overseer of New Life Church in Colorado Springs, Colorado.

Jimmy served as the senior pastor of Trinity Fellowship Church in Amarillo, Texas, for 30 years and now serves as the senior elder. During his years of leadership, Trinity grew from 900 active members to over 10,000.

He holds an honorary doctorate of literature from The Kings University and has authored more than 16 books, among which are his popular works *Marriage on the Rock, Ten Steps Toward Christ, Lifelong Love*

Affair, When Life Hurts, Strengths Based Marriage, and *I Changed My Mind.*

Jimmy and Karen have been married for 45 years and have two married children and five grandchildren.

JIMMY EVANS

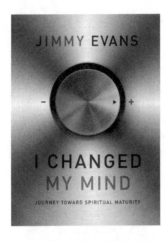

Next to salvation, changing your thinking may have the single greatest impact on your life. **Change your mind. Change your life.**

ISBN: 9781945529320
eBook ISBN: 9781945529337
Spanish ISBN: 9781945529344

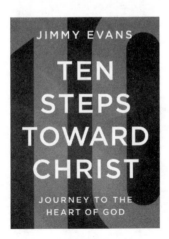

Salvation isn't the last step. It's the first.
Jimmy Evans gives you a map to navigate your new life through down-to-earth principles.

ISBN: 9781945529252
eBook ISBN: 9781945529269
Spanish ISBN: 9781945529276

You can find these Jimmy Evans resources at the Gateway Bookstore and wherever Christian books are sold.

A Note on the Type

This book was typeset in Chronicle Text G3. Chronicle Text is a typeface designed by Hoefler & Co. in 2002. A Scotch styled typeface, Chronicle Text blends the best of both Old Style serif fonts and Modern serif fonts. The typeface was originally designed for newspapers and was created in several grades including G3.

Typeset by Nord Compo,
Villeneuve-d'Ascq, France

Printed and bound by Lake Book Manufacturing,
Melrose Park, Illinois

Interior design by Peyton Sepeda